Poetry By English Women

Elizabethan to Victorian

*Edited with an Introduction and Notes
by R. E. Pritchard*

Continuum · New York

For

Susan, John and Anna

1993

The Continuum Publishing Company
370 Lexington Avenue, New York, NY 10017

Printed in the United States of America

Library of Congress Cataloging-in-Publication Data

    Poetry by English women : Elizabethan to Victorian / edited with
an introduction and notes by R.E. Pritchard.
      p.   cm.
    Originally published: English women's poetry. Manchester, England
 : Carcanet Press, 1990
    Includes bibliographical references (p.) and index.
    ISBN 0-8264-0599-1 (pbk.)
    1. English poetry—Women authors.   2. Women—England—Poetry.
I. Pritchard, R. E.
[PR1117.E54   1993]
821.008'09287—dc20   93-20688
                                                    CIP

Contents

7

10

An asterisk by the title in the text indicates that there are notes to the poem at the end of the book.

Acknowledgements

The editor and publishers gratefully acknowledge permission to use copyright material in this book as follows:

Mary Coleridge: reprinted from *The Collected Poems of Mary Coleridge*, edited by Theresa Whistler (Rupert Hart-Davis, 1954), by permission of the editor.

Elizabeth I: reprinted from *The Poems of Queen Elizabeth I*, edited by Leicester Bradner, by permission of the University Press of New England. Copyright © 1984 by Brown University.

Mary (Sidney) Herbert: reprinted from *The Psalms of Sir Philip Sidney and the Countess of Pembroke*, edited by J.C.A. Rathmell, by permission of New York University Press.

Emilia Lanyer: reprinted from *The Poems of Shakespeare's Dark Lady*, edited by A.L. Rowse (Jonathan Cape, 1978), by permission of the editor.

Mary Wortley Montagu: reprinted from *Lady Mary Wortley Montagu: Essays and Poems*, edited by Robert Halsband and Isobel Grundy (Clarendon Press, 1977), by permission of Isobel Grundy.

Dorothy Wordsworth: reprinted from *Dorothy Wordsworth and Romanticism* by Susan M. Levin, by permission of Rutgers State University Press and the Wordsworth Trust, Dove Cottage, Grasmere.

Mary Wroth: reprinted by permission of Louisiana State University Press from *The Poems of Lady Mary Wroth*, edited by Josephine A. Roberts. Copyright © 1983 Louisiana State University Press.

Every effort has been made to secure permission to include the poems in this anthology; the editor and publishers would be grateful for notification of any omissions or corrections.

Introduction

An anthologist of women's poetry from the sixteenth to the nineteenth century has the pleasure and advantage of dealing with relatively little-known poetry, of a remarkably wide range – here are to be found both love-song and feminist polemic, witty satire and religious rhapsody, bawdy fun and grave meditation. Not everyone might approve of an anthology deliberately confined to writers of one sex, but the fact is that far too few ordinary readers and students have been able to get a fair sense of the variety and vitality of English women's poetry over these centuries. Quite simply, there are some very good poems in here, and some remarkable poets, that should be better known. Yet, often, it has hardly been apparent that they were there at all. Apart from a handful of the romanticized famous, even the more considerable have had to wait until fairly recently for sound editions, let alone general recognition. To some extent, of course, it has been cultural prejudice (conscious or unconscious, and shared by women) that has led to women poets' near-absence from the standard, period anthologies (though that is now becoming less the case); partly they were elbowed out by the acknowledged major authors, partly not recognized by a taste unfamiliar with feminine attitudes and themes. Here, at any rate, is a selection, made not to illustrate any thesis, but simply to bring together some lively and engaging poems that should appeal to many modern readers, and provide an introduction to an important and neglected element in English poetic history.

We need to extend our sense of the history or pattern of English poetry, to bring in the overlooked. There is no one canon of English poetry – rather, a constantly shifting set of engagements and valuations produced by changing responses to contemporary life: as we see the present differently, so we cannot but see the past differently. An apparent absence proves not to have been a vacancy: muted voices become audible, individual, various, in a dialect different but recognizable and intriguing.

In this volume, spelling and typographic conventions regarding the use of capitals, italics and so on, have been brought into line with modern usage (though punctuation is usually unchanged); while this makes for greater accessibility, one should not forget what varying appearances suggest – that different linguistic usages are inseparable from changing cultures and assumptions. We are dealing with products of a patriarchal society evolving over some four hundred years. It is important to remember how much our experiences, and the words for them, are culturally shaped and conditioned: friendship, 'love, marriage, husband, wife, home – all have had different significances, for both sexes at different times. We should not read these poems assuming that their writers felt quite what we might feel with or through their words. Their voices echo out of the past: though the experiences and responses are recognizable, we may not catch everything they say.

Obviously, the primary psychological development of the sexes differs, producing different conceptions of interiority, identity and relationships. Even though these are partially products of the orderings developed through the shared language, one must recognize that access to and usage of these discourses is not the same for men and women. Whole ranges of behaviour – linguistic, social, sexual, economic – have been unavailable to women, virtually unthinkable, precluded by various circumstances: lack of education, religious or class proscriptions or inhibitions, assumptions of innate incapacity, as well as, for many, by lack of time, money or access. Necessarily this has affected attitudes to writing, both fundamentally – as to whether one writes, or why, or for whom – and more obviously, in relation to conventions that are gender-oriented, such as Renaissance Petrarchist love-poetry, or Romantic myths of Mother Nature. The cultural myths, concerns and changes of their times appear in women's verse, but often differently, or indirectly. Women might be seen as constituting a major social grouping within the changing cultures of their times, with – like other groupings – varying access to and representation in the discourses of those times, and with varying degrees of awareness of constituting such a group (awareness of other affinities, such as of class or religion, sometimes being more significant). One cannot readily speak of a tradition of women's poetry during these years – writers would need a stronger sense of a common pursuit among predecessors and contemporaries – let alone a movement, except perhaps towards the end, though some continuities and developments might be traced. Some common themes do appear in women's poetry, of course – friendship between women; complaints against male dominance, with demands for equality and self-determination; love (variously understood); children; domestic life; sympathy with oppressed groups; the necessity of self-expression (or is it self-creation?) through writing – but changing in emphasis with changing circumstances.

The Renaissance humanist tradition of the educated lady is represented here by Queen Elizabeth, Mary Herbert and Mary Wroth: religious or moral writing was all that might be approved for ladies then; courtiers might write for self-advertisement and career advancement, but such objectives were in any case inappropriate or irrelevant to the women. The lower orders were rarely literate, with necessarily limited horizons: Isabella Whitney's education and literary ambitions were both very unusual. Social tension about gender roles and women's position developed during the earlier seventeenth century, as other social, religious and political strains increased; merchant-class Nonconformity was to prove beneficial to women's interests, in encouraging literacy for independent Bible study, while devotional and 'prophetic' writing flourished (one might think of An Collins, or Anne Bradstreet); the Civil War provided many occasions for self-assertion, as Margaret Cavendish's activities might suggest. The Restoration's brief openness to personal, economic and sexual expression, and new demand for entertainment, were in practice mixed blessings. Sexual activity was flaunted (Behn, Ephelia, Pilkington – Montagu: but she was an aristocrat, and could get away with it!), but also provoked prim reactions, whereby it became even less respectable for ladies to publish (Cavendish was derided, Philips, Ephelia and Finch all published pseudonymously). For some years, the theme of women's rights in the face of husbands' absolute powers became almost a minor genre, to be exercised by any self-respecting woman writer (Chudleigh, Elizabeth Tollet), before the blanket of Whig complacency settled down.

The eighteenth century saw increasing numbers of middle-class women taking up writing – especially of novels (Charlotte Smith) – to satisfy the growing numbers of literate and (involuntarily) leisured women of that class, actually discouraged from independent activity and increasingly confined to a private, domestic life, subject to growing cults of motherhood and refined manners. Some, such as Mary Jones, or Fanny Burney, associated themselves with important male writers, such as Pope, Richardson and Johnson; others with ladies' literary and philanthropic groups, producing Popean satire or sympathy with the deserving oppressed – slaves, chimney-sweeps, lower-class women writers (such as Leapor and the milk-woman poet Ann Yearsley) – while discouraging serious social questioning (Hannah More). The lower orders, trapped by poor education and by hard labour away from home, in agriculture, domestic service or the mills, produced the social complaint (Collier). The Nonconformist, progressive tradition continued to be one of major and increasing importance for women writers (Barbauld, Taylor)

The literary lady became increasingly established (More, Barbauld, Hemans); from the Restoration onwards, women poets were not neglected by reviewers, and many – More, Hemans, Adelaide Procter (reputedly Queen Victoria's favourite poet), Ingelow – sold very well, while others – Barbauld, Barrett Browning – won considerable intellectual respect. However, pressures for respectability, sublimation and self-repression also flourished, with smothering and distorting effects (in three different ways, Hemans, Wordsworth, Rossetti). Political and intellectual developments associated with, for example, Mary Wollstonecraft, Mme de Staël and Rousseau, together with Romantic attitudes to Nature, the will and imagination, motivated and unsettled others (Barrett Browning, the Brontës) – the imagination and sexuality merging unnervingly. Many, of course, worked within Victorian values of optimism and good works (Procter, Ingelow, Greenwell – where a sublimated sexual energy is discernible); some indeed, effaced their female identities, almost subversively, behind male pseudonyms: Currer Bell, Michael Field, George Eliot. Nevertheless, as the century proceeds, a more independently feminine, and even feminist voice and sensibility become apparent. A repressive social orthodoxy provoked increasingly a melancholy, even morbid note in women's verse (preceding, if later merging with, *fin de siècle* sentiment); sometimes this is lost in the liberating energy of radical and suffragist movements (Guggenberger, Mathilde Blind, Meynell), sometimes, a deeper alienation is suggested (Levy, Coleridge).

With Mary Coleridge the volume concludes, on the brink of the great development in women's self-awareness, associated with suffragist and feminist movements, and the enormous expansion and flourishing of women's poetry in this century. That, too great for inclusion in this volume, is well represented elsewhere. Regrettably, many interesting poets have had to be excluded – yet again; but for these writers, mostly 'too little and too lately known', here are some indications of what they were capable of, and of where more may be found.

Further Reading

Some anthologies of English women's poetry of this period:
Alexander Dyce (ed), *Specimens of British Poetesses* (London: T. Rodd, 1827).

J.C. Squire (ed), *A Book of Women's Verse* (Oxford: Clarendon, 1921).

Betty Travitsky (ed), *The Paradise of Women: Writings by Englishwomen of the Renaissance* (Westport, Conn: Greenwood, 1981).

Germaine Greer, Jeslyn Medoff, Melinda Sansone and Susan Hastings (eds), *Kissing the Rod: An Anthology of Seventeenth Century Women's Verse,* (London: Virago, 1988)

Dale Spender and Janet Todd (eds), *Anthology of British Women Writers,* (London: Pandora, 1989).

Roger Lonsdale (ed), *Eighteenth Century Women Poets: An Oxford Anthology, (Oxford: OUP, 1989).*

Some recent critical and historical introductions:
Sandra M. Gilbert and Susan Gubar (eds), *Shakespeare's Sisters: Feminist Essays on Women Poets* (Bloomington and London: Indiana UP, 1979).

Elaine Showalter (ed), *The New Feminist Criticism: Essays on Women, Literature and Theory* (NY: Pantheon, 1985).

Margaret Homans, *Bearing the Word: Language and Female Experience in Nineteenth-Century Women's Writing* (Chicago: Chicago UP, 1986).

Elaine V. Beilin, *Redeeming Eve: Women Writers of the English Renaissance (Princeton: Princeton UP, 1987).*

Jan Montefiore, *Feminism and Poetry: Language, Experience, Identity in Women's Writing* (London and NY: Pandora, 1987).

Elaine Hobby, *Virtue of Necessity: English Women's Writing 1649-88,* (London: Virago, 1988).

Janet Todd, *Feminist Literary History: A Defence* (Cambridge: Polity, 1988).

Janet Todd (ed), *Dictionary of British Women Writers* (London: Routledge, 1989).

QUEEN ELIZABETH I
1533-1603

The daughter of King Henry VIII and Anne Boleyn; succeeded her half-brother, Edward VI, and her half-sister, Mary I, to the throne in 1558. Highly educated, and proficient in Latin (she also translated Boethius) and four foreign languages, an eloquent speaker and consummate politician. The focus of political and erotic ambition, and of a quasi-religious cult of 'the Virgin Queen', she depended for security on remaining single (*'Semper eadem, semper una'*, as in her motto).

Leicester Bradner (ed), *Poems of Queen Elizabeth I* (Providence, R.I: Brown UP, 1964; Paul Johnson, *Elizabeth I: A Study of Power and Intellect* (London: Weidenfeld and Nicolson, 1974).

Written with a Diamond
On her Window at Woodstock*

Much suspected by me,
Nothing proved can be,
           Quoth Elizabeth prisoner.

Written on a Wall at Woodstock

Oh, fortune, thy wresting wavering state
Hath fraught with cares my troubled wit,
Whose witness this present prison late
Could bear, where once was joy's loan quit.
Thou causedst the guilty to be loosed
From bands where innocents were inclosed,
And caused the guiltless to be reserved,
And freed those that death had well deserved.
But all herein can be nothing wrought,
So God send to my foes all they have thought.   **10**

Written in her French Psalter

No crooked leg, no bleared eye,
  No part deformed out of kind,
No yet so ugly half can be
  As is the inward suspicious mind.

The Doubt of Future Foes*

The doubt of future foes exiles my present joy,
And wit warns me to shun such snares as threaten mine
      annoy;
For falsehood now doth flow, and subjects' faith doth ebb,
Which should not be if reason ruled or wisdom weaved the
      web.
But clouds of joys untried do cloak aspiring minds,
Which turn to rain of late repent by changed course of
      winds.
The top of hope supposed the root upreared shall be,
And fruitless all their grafted guile, as shortly ye shall see.
The dazzled eyes with pride, which great ambition blinds,
Shall be unsealed by worthy wights whose foresight
      falsehood finds.   10
The daughter of debate that discord aye doth sow
Shall reap no gain where former rule still peace hath taught
      to know.
No foreign banished wight shall anchor in this port;
Our realm brooks not seditious sects, let them elsewhere
      resort.
My rusty sword through rest shall first his edge employ
To poll their tops that seek such change or gape for future joy.

On Monsieur's Departure*

I grieve and dare not show my discontent,
I love and yet am forced to seem to hate,
I do, yet dare not say I ever meant,
I seem stark mute but inwardly do prate.
   I am and am not, I freeze and yet am burned,
   Since from myself another self I turned.

My care is like my shadow in the sun,
Follows me flying, flies when I pursue it,
Stands and lies by me, doth what I have done.
His too familiar care doth make me rue it.   10
   No means I find to rid him from my breast,
   Till by the end of things it be suppressed.

Some gentler passion slide into my mind,
For I am soft and made of melting snow;
Or be more cruel, love, and so be kind.
Let me float or sink, be high or low.
   Or let me live with some more sweet content,
   Or die and so forget what love e'er meant.

ISABELLA WHITNEY

fl. 1567

The first Englishwoman to publish her own verses. Possibly the sister of Geoffrey Whitney, emblematist and versifier, of Coole Pilate, Cheshire, though she herself was London bred. Socially, the family seems to have been on the lower fringes of the middle class. Reasonably well-read in the popular classics, especially Ovid; writes mostly in the plain style's method of long-winded, accumulative illustration, the anthologist's bane. Wrote verse epistles on faithlessness in love, and sober advice to her family; the *Nosegay* is mostly versification of moral aphorisms in Hugh Plat's *Flowers of Philosophie,* derived from Seneca. Her career, even if not wholly successful, seems to suggest that disaster might not have been as inevitable for 'Shakespeare's sister' as Virginia Woolf suggested. In this selection, punctuation also has been modernized.

The Copy of a letter, lately written in meeter, by a yonge Gentilwoman: to her unconstant lover (London 1567); *A sweet nosegay or pleasant posye. Contayning a hundred and ten Phylosophicall flowres* (London, 1573); Betty Travitsky, 'The "Wyll and Testament" of Isabella Whitney', *English Literary Review* 10 (1980) pp.76-95.

From *The admonition by the Auctor to all yong Gentilwomen: And to al other Maids being in Love*

Ye virgins that from Cupid's tents
    do bear away the foil,
Whose hearts as yet with raging love
    most painfully do boil,

To you I speak: for you be they
    that good advice do lack.
Oh, if I could good counsel give
    my tongue should not be slack.

But such as I can give, I will
    here in few words express,   10

Which if you do observe, it will
    some of your care redress.

Beware of fair and painted talk,
    beware of flattering tongues:
The mermaids do pretend no good
    for all their pleasant songs.

Some use the tears of crocodiles,
    contrary to their heart,
And if they cannot always weep,
    they wet their cheeks by art.   20

Ovid, within his *Art of Love*,
    doth teach them this same knack
To wet their hand, and touch their eyes,
    so oft as tears they lack.

Why have you such deceit in store?
    have you such crafty wile?
Less craft than this God knows would soon
    us simple souls beguile.

And will ye not leave off? but still
    delude us in this wise?   30
Sith it is so, we trust we shall
    take heed to feigned lies.

Trust not a man at the first sight,
    but try him well before:
I wish all maids within their breasts
    to keep this thing in store.

For trial shall declare his truth,
    and show what he doth think,
Whether he be a lover true,
    or do intend to shrink . [. . .]   40

Hero did try Leander's truth,
 before that she did trust:
Therefore she found him unto her
 both constant, true, and just.

For he always did swim the sea
 when stars in sky did glide,
Till he was drowned by the way
 near hand unto the side.

She scrat her face, she tare her hair
 (it grieveth me to tell)   50
When she did know the end of him
 that she did love so well.

But like Leander there be few,
 therefore in time take heed,
And always try before you trust,
 so shall you better speed.

The little fish that careless is
 within the water clear:
How glad is he, when he doth see
 a bait for to appear.   60

He thinks his hap right good to be,
 that he the same could spy,
And so the simple fool doth trust
 too much before he try.

O little fish what hap hadst thou,
 to have such spiteful fate,
To come into one's cruel hands,
 out of so happy state:

Thou didst suspect no harm, when thou
 upon the bait did look: 70

O that thou hadst Linceus' eyes
    for to have seen the hook.

Then hadst thou with thy pretty mates
    been playing in the streams,
Whereas Sir Phoebus daily doth
    show forth his golden beams.

But sith thy fortune is so ill,
    to end thy life on shore:
Of this thy most unhappy end
    I mind to speak no more,   80

But of thy fellow's chance that late
    such pretty shaft did make
That he from fisher's hook did sprint
    before he could him take.

And now he pries on every bait,
    suspecting still that prick
For to lie in every thing,
    Wherewith the fishers strike.

And since the fish, that reason lacks,
    once warned, doth beware: 90
Why should not we take heed to that
    that turneth us to care.

And I who was deceived late,
    by one's unfaithful tears,
Trust now for to be ware, if that
    I live this hundred years.

FINIS.   Is.W.

Wyll and Testament*
[on having to leave London]

The time is come I must depart
    from thee oh famous City:
I never yet, to rue my smart,
    did find that thou hadst pity.
Wherefore small cause there is, that I
    should grieve from thee to go:
But many women foolishly,
    like me, and other moe,
Do such a fixed fancy set
    on those which least deserve,   10
That long it is ere wit we get
    away from them to swerve [. . .]
And now hath time put me in mind
    of thy great cruelness,
That never once a help would find,
    to ease me in distress [. . .]
No, no, thou never didst me good,
    nor ever wilt, I know:
Yet I am in no angry mood,
    but will, or ere I go,   20
In perfect love and charity,
    my testament here write,
And leave to thee such treasury
    as I in it recite.
Now stand aside and give me leave
    to write my latest will,
And see that none you do deceive,
    of that I leave them til. [. . .]
I whole in body, and in mind,
    but very weak in purse   30
Do make, and write my testament
    for fear it will be worse. [. . .]
I first of all to London leave,
because I there was bred,

Brave buildings rare, of churches store,
   and Paul's to the head . [. . .]
Watling Street and Canwyck Street
   I full of woollen leave,
And linen store in Friday Street,
   if they me not deceive.   40
And those which are of calling such,
   that costlier they require,
I mercers leave, with silk so rich,
   as any would desire.
In Cheap of them, they store shall find,
   and likewise in that street,
I goldsmiths leave, with jewels such
   as are for ladies meet.
And plate to furnish cupboards with,
   full brave there you shall find,   50
With purl of silver and of gold,
   to satisfy your mind.
With hoods, bongraces, hats or caps,
   such store are in that street,
As if on t'one side you should miss,
   the tother serves you for't . [. . .]
For women shall you tailors have,
   by Bow the chiefest dwell:
In every lane you some shall find,
   can do indifferent well.   60
And for the men, few streets or lanes
   but body-makers be,
And such as make the sweeping cloaks,
   with gardes beneath the knee.
Artillery at Temple Bar,
   and dagges at Tower Hill;
Swords and bucklers of the best
   are nigh the Fleet until . [. . .]
At Steelyard store of wines there be,
   your dulled minds to glad,   70
And handsome men, that must not wed

except they leave their trade.
They oft shall seek for proper girls,
   and some perhaps shall find
That need compels, or lucre lures,
   to satisfy their mind.
And near the same, I houses leave
   for people to repair,
To bathe themselves, so to prevent
   infection of the air . [. . .]   80
And that the poor, when I am gone,
   have cause for me to pray,
I will to prisons portions leave,
   what though but very small:
Yet that they may remember me,
   occasion be it shall . [. . .]
The Newgate once a month shall have
   a sessions for his share,
Lest, being heaped, infection might
   procure a further care.   90
And at those sessions some shall 'scape
   with burning near the thumb,
And afterward to beg their fees,
   till they have got the sum . [. . .]
To all the bookbinders by Paul's
   because I like their art,
They every week shall money have,
   when they from books depart . [. . .]
For maidens poor, I widowers rich
   do leave, that oft shall dote,   100
And by that means shall marry them,
   to set the girls afloat.
And wealthy widows will I leave,
   to help yong gentlemen,
Which when you have, in any case
   be courteous to them then,
And see their plate and jewels eke
   may not be marred with rust,

Nor let their bags too long be full,
    for fear that they do burst . [. . .]   110
To Smithfield I must something leave,
    my parents there did dwell:
So careless for to be of it,
    none would account it well.
Wherefore it thrice a week shall have
    of horse and neat good store,
And in his Spital, blind and lame
    to dwell for evermore.
And Bedlam must not be forgot,
    for that was oft my walk: 120
I people there too many leave,
    That out of tune do talk.
At Bridewell there shall beadles be,
    and Matrons that shall still
See chalk well chopped, and spinning plied,
    and turning of the mill . [. . .]
And also leave I at each Inn
    of Court, or Chancery,
Of gentlemen, a youthful rout,
    full of activity,   130
For whom I store of books have left,
    at each bookbinder's stall
And part of all that London hath
    to furnish them withal.
And when they are with study cloyed,
    to recreate their mind,
Of tennis courts, of dancing schools,
    and fence, they store shall find.
And every Sunday at the least,
    I leave to make them sport,   140
In divers places players, that
    Of wonders shall report.
Now London have I, for thy sake,
    within thee, and without,
As come into my memory,

    dispersed round about
Such needful things, as they should have
    here left now unto thee:
When I am gone, with conscience
    let them dispersed be . [. . .]   150
This xx. of October I,
    in ANNO DOMINI:
A thousand v. hundred seventy three,
    as almanacs do descry,
Did write this will with mine own hand
    and it to London gave:
In witness of the standers-by,
    whose name, if you will have,
Paper, pen and standish were,
    at that time present by,   160
With Time, who promised to reveal,
    so fast as she could hie,
The same, lest of my nearer kin
    for any thing should vary.
So finally I make an end,
    no longer can I tarry.
FINIS.   by Is. W

LADY MARY HERBERT,
COUNTESS OF PEMBROKE
1561-1621

'She was a beautiful Ladie and had an excellent witt, and had the best breeding that that age could afford. Shee had a pritty sharpe-ovall face. Her haire was of a reddish yellowe ...She was the greatest Patronesse of witt and learning of any Lady in her time ...there was so great love between [Sir Philip Sidney] and his faire sister that I have heard old Gentlemen say that they lay together': thus, characteristically, Aubrey in his *Brief Lives*. The fifth child of Sir Henry and Lady Mary Sidney, of Penshurst Place in Kent; in 1577 married Henry Herbert, Earl of Pembroke (then aged over forty); lived at Wilton near Salisbury and had three children. An important literary patron, she also oversaw the post-humous publication of her brother's writings, translated, wrote a little verse of her own, and, most important, collaborated with Philip in trans-lating the Psalms, completing the bulk of the work after his death. The psalms, described as her work of self-discovery as a poet, were widely praised and influential.

J.C.A. Rathmell (ed), *The Psalms of Sir Philip Sidney and the Countess of Pembroke* (NY: NYUP, 1963); Elaine V. Beilin, *Redeeming Eve: Women Writers of the English Renaissance* (Princeton: Princeton UP, 1987); Rivkah Zim, *English Metrical Psalms: Poetry as Praise and Prayer, 1535-1601* (Cambridge: CUP, 1987); Michael G. Brennan, *Literary Patronage in the Renaissance: The Pembroke Family* (London: Routledge, 1988).

Psalm 57: Miserere Mei, Deus

Thy mercy, Lord, Lord now thy mercy show,
    On thee I lie
    To thee I fly
  Hide me, hive me as thine own,
  Till these blasts be overblown,
Which now do fiercely blow.

To the highest God I will erect my cry,
    Who quickly shall

Dispatch this all.
He shall from Heaven send   10
From disgrace me to defend,
His love and verity.

My soul encaged lies with lions' brood,
    Villains whose hands
    Are fiery brands,
Teeth more sharp than shaft or spear,
Tongues far better edge do bear
Than swords to shed my blood.

As high as highest heav'n can give thee place,
    O Lord ascend,   20
    And thence extend
With most bright, most glorious show,
Over all the earth below
The sun-beams of thy face.

Me to entangle, ev'ry way I go,
    Their trap and net
    Is ready set.
Holes they dig, but their own holes
Pitfalls make for their own souls:
So Lord, O serve them so.   30

My heart prepar'd, prepared is my heart
    To spread thy praise
    With tuned lays:
Wake my tongue, my lute awake,
Thou my harp the consort make,
My self will bear a part.

My self when first the morning shall appear,
    With voice and string
    So will thee sing:
That this earthly globe, and all   40

Treading on this earthly ball,
My praising notes shall hear.

For God, my only God, thy gracious love
    Is mounted far
    Above each star,
   Thy unchanged verity
   Heav'nly wings do lift as high
As clouds have room to move.

As high as highest heav'n can give thee place
    O Lord ascend   50
    And thence extend
   With most bright, most glorious show
   Over all the earth below,
The sun-beams of thy face.

Psalm 58: Si Vere Utique*

And call ye this to utter what is just,
   You that of justice hold the sov'reign throne?
And call ye this to yield, O sons of dust,
   To wronged brethren ev'ry man his own?
O no; it is your long malicious will
   Now to the world to make by practice known,
With whose oppression you the balance fill,
   Just to your selves, indiff'rent else to none.
But what could they, who ev'n in birth declin'd,
   From truth and right to lies and injuries?   10
To show the venom of their cankered mind
   The adder's image scarcely can suffice;
Nay scarce the aspic may with them contend,
   On whom the charmer all in vain applies
His skilfull'st spells: ay missing of his end,
   While she self-deaf, and unaffected lies.

Lord crack their teeth, Lord crush these lions' jaws,
    So let them sink as water in the sand:
When deadly bow their aiming fury draws
    Shiver the shaft ere past the shooter's hand.   20
So make them melt as the dishoused snail
    Or as the embryo, whose vital band
Breaks ere it holds, and formless eyes do fail
    To see the sun, though brought to lightful land.
O let their brood, a brood of springing thorns,
    Be by untimely rooting overthrown
Ere bushes waxed, they push with pricking horns,
    As fruits yet green are oft by tempest blown.
The good with gladness this revenge shall see,
    And bathe his feet in blood of wicked one   30
While all shall say: the just rewarded be,
    There is a God that carves to each his own.

Psalm 92: Bonum Est Confiteri

O lovely thing
To sing and praises frame
To thee, O Lord, and thy high name;
    With early spring
    Thy bounty to display,
Thy truth when night hath vanquished day:
    Yea so to sing,
    That ten-stringed instrument
With lute, and harp, and voice consent.

    For, Lord, my mind   10
    Thy works with wonder fill;
Thy doings are my comfort still.
    What wit can find,
    How bravely thou hast wrought,

Or deeply sound thy shallow'st thought?
　　　The fool is blind,
　　And blindly doth not know,
How like the grass the wicked grow.

　　　The wicked grow
　　Like frail though flow'ry grass;   20
And fall'n, to wrack past help do pass.
　　　But thou not so,
　　But high thou still dost stay:
And lo thy haters fall away.
　　　Thy haters lo,
　　Decay and perish all;
All wicked hands to ruin fall.

　　　Fresh oiled I
　　Will lively lift my horn,
And match the matchless unicorn: 30
　　　Mine eye shall spy
　　My spies in spiteful case;
Mine ear shall hear my foes' disgrace.
　　　Like cedar high
　　And like date-bearing tree,
For green, and growth the just shall be.

　　　Where God doth dwell
　　Shall be his spreading place:
God's courts shall his fair boughs embrace.
　　　Even then shall swell   40
　　His blossoms fat and fair,
When aged rind the stock shall bear.
　　　And I shall tell
　　How God my Rock is just,
So just, with him is nought unjust.

Psalm 139: Domine, Probasti*

O Lord in me there lieth nought,
  But to thy search revealed lies:
    For when I sit
    Thou markest it:
  No less thou notest when I rise:
Yea closest closet of my thought
  Hath open windows to thine eyes.

Thou walkest with me when I walk,
  When to my bed for rest I go,
    I find thee there,   10
    And ev'ry where:
  Not youngest thought in me doth grow,
No not one word I cast to talk,
  But yet unuttered thou dost know.

If forth I march, thou goest before,
  If back I turn, thou com'st behind:
    So forth nor back
    Thy guard I lack,
  Nay on me too, thy hand I find.
Well I thy wisdom may adore,   20
But never reach with earthy mind.

To shun thy notice, leave thine eye,
  O whither might I take my way?
    To starry sphere?
    Thy throne is there.
  To dead men's undelightsome stay?
There is thy walk, and there to lie
  Unknown, in vain I should assay.

O sun, whom light nor flight can match,
  Suppose thy lightful flightful wings   30
    Thou lend to me,

And I could flee
As far as thee the ev'ning brings:
Ev'n led to West he would me catch,
Nor should I lurk with western things.

Do thou thy best, O secret night,
In sable veil to cover me:
Thy sable veil
Shall vainly fail:
With day unmasked my night shall be,   40
For night is day, and darkness light,
O father of all lights, to thee.

Each inmost piece in me is thine:
While yet I in my mother dwelt,
All that me clad
From thee I had.
Thou in my frame hast strangely dealt:
Needs in my praise thy works must shine
So inly them my thoughts have felt.

Thou, how my back was beam-wise laid,   50
And raft'ring of my ribs, dost know:
Know'st ev'ry point
Of bone and joint,
How to this whole these parts did grow,
In brave embroid'ry fair arrayed,
Though wrought in shop both dark and low.

Nay fashionless, ere form I took,
Thy all and more beholding eye
My shapeless shape
Could not escape: 60
All these time framed successively
Ere one had being, in the book
Of thy foresight, enrolled did lie.

My God, how I these studies prize,
　　That do thy hidden workings show!
　　　　Whose sum is such,
　　　　No sum so much:
　　Nay summed as sand they sumless grow.
I lie to sleep, from sleep I rise,
　　Yet still in thought with thee I go.　　　　　　　　70

My God if thou but one wouldst kill,
　　Then straight would leave my further chase
　　　　This cursed brood
　　　　Inured to blood:
　　Whose graceless taunts at thy disgrace
Have aimed oft: and hating still
　　Would with proud lies thy truth outface.

Hate not I them, who thee do hate?
　　Thine, Lord, I will the censure be.
　　　　Detest I not　　　　　　　　　　　　　　80
　　　　The cankered knot,
　　Whom I against thee banded see?
O Lord, thou know'st in highest rate
　　I hate them all as foes to me.

Search me, my God, and prove my heart,
　　Examine me, and try my thought:
　　　　And mark in me
　　　　If aught there be
　　That hath with cause their anger wrought.
If not (as not) my life's each part,　　　　　　　　90
　　Lord safely guide from danger brought.

EMILIA LANYER (or LANIER)
1569-1645

The illegitimate daughter of an Italian royal musician, Baptista Bassano, and Margaret Johnson; mistress of the Lord Chancellor, Lord Hunsdon and, when pregnant, married off to Alphonso Lanier, another royal musician. A.L. Rowse suggested she was Shakespeare's mistress; in 1597-1600, was involved with the astrologer Simon Forman, who described her as 'high-minded ... very brave in youth... many false conceptions... for lucre's sake will be a good fellow'. She worked her aristocratic connections: her 1611 volume has ten dedications to the Queen and aristocratic ladies, notably to Margaret, the Dowager Countess of Cumberland, the real object of the exercise. Of the title poem, *Salve Deus Rex Iudaeorum*, ostensibly celebrating Christ, about half actually celebrates Biblical heroines and contemporary ladies, notably the Countess, once apologizing for digressing from her praise to that of Christ.

A.L. Rowse (ed. and intro.), *The Poems of Shakespeare's Dark Lady: 'Salve Deus Rex Iudaeorum'* (London: Jonathan Cape, 1978).

The Description of Cooke-ham*

Farewell (sweet Cookeham) where I first obtained
Grace from that Grace where perfect grace remained;
And where the Muses gave their full consent,
I should have pow'r the virtuous to content:
Where princely palace willed me to endite,
The sacred story of the soul's delight.
Farewell (sweet place) where virtue then did rest,
And all delights did harbour in her breast:
Never shall my sad eyes again behold
Those pleasures which my thoughts did then unfold: 10
Yet you (great Lady) mistress of that place,
From whose desires did spring this work of grace;
Vouchsafe to think upon those pleasures past,
As fleeting worldly joys that could not last:

Or, as dim shadows of celestial pleasures,
Which are desired above all earthly treasures.
Oh how (methought) against you thither came,
Each part did seem some new delight to frame!
The House received all ornaments to grace it,
And would endure no foulness to deface it.   20
The walks put on their summer liveries,
And all things else did hold like similes:
The trees with leaves, with fruits, with flowers clad,
Embraced each other, seeming to be glad,
Turning themselves to beauteous canopies,
To shade the bright sun from your brighter eyes:
The crystal streams with silver spangles graced,
While by the glorious sun they were embraced:
The little birds in chirping notes did sing,
To entertain both you and that sweeet spring.   30
And Philomela with her sundry lays,
Both you and that delightful place did praise.
Oh how methought each plant, each flow'r, each tree
Set forth their beauties then to welcome thee:
The very hills right humbly did descend ,
When you to tread upon them did intend.
And as you set your feet, they still did rise,
Glad that they could receive so rich a prize.
The gentle winds did take delight to be
Among those woods that were so graced by thee.   40
And in sad murmur uttered pleasing sound,
That pleasure in that place might more abound:
The swelling banks delivered all their pride,
When such a phoenix once they had espied.
Each arbour, bank, each seat, each stately tree,
Thought themselves honoured in supporting thee.
The pretty birds would oft come to attend thee,
Yet fly away for fear they should offend thee:
The little creatures in the burrow by
Would come abroad to sport them in your eye;   50
Yet fearful of the bow in your fair hand,

Would run away when you did make a stand.
Now let me come unto that stately tree,
Wherein such goodly prospects you did see;
That oak that did in height his fellows pass,
As much as lofty trees, low growing grass:
Much like a comely cedar straight and tall,
Whose beauteous stature far exceeded all:
How often did you visit this fair tree,
Which seeming joyful in receiving thee,   60
Would like a palm tree spread his arms abroad,
Desirous that you there should make abode;
Whose fair green leaves much like a comely veil,
Defended Phoebus when he would assail:
Whose pleasing boughs did yield a cool fresh air,
Joying his happiness when you were there.
Where being seated, you might plainly see,
Hills, vales, and woods, as if on bended knee
They had appeared, your honour to salute,
Or to prefer some strange unlooked-for suit: 70
All interlaced with brooks and crystal springs,
A prospect fit to please the eyes of kings:
And thirteen shires appeared all in your sight,
Europe could not afford much more delight.
What was there then but gave you all content,
While you the time in meditation spent,
Of their Creator's pow'r, which there you saw,
In all his creatures held a perfect law;
And in their beauties did you plain descry,
His beauty, wisdom, grace, love, majesty.   80
In these sweet woods how often did you walk,
With Christ and his Apostles there to talk;
Placing his holy writ in some fair tree,
To meditate what you therein did see:
With Moses did you mount his holy hill,
To know his pleasure, and perform his will.
With lovely David you did often sing,
His holy hymns to Heaven's eternal king.

41

And in sweet music did your soul delight,
To sound his praises, morning, noon, and night.   90
With blessed Joseph you did often feed
Your pined brethren, when they stood in need.
And that sweet Lady sprung from Clifford's race,
Of noble Bedford's blood, fair stream of grace;
To honourable Dorset now espoused,
In whose fair breast true virtue then was housed:
Oh what delight did my weak spirits find
In those pure parts of her well framed mind:
And yet it grieves me that I cannot be
Near unto her, whose virtues did agree   100
With those fair ornaments of outward beauty,
Which did enforce from all both love and duty.
Unconstant Fortune, thou art most to blame,
Who casts us down into so low a frame:
Where our great friends we cannot daily see,
So great a diff'rence is there in degree.
Many are placed in those orbs of state,
Nearer in show, yet farther off in love,
In which, the lowest always are above.   110
But whither I am carried in conceit?
My wit too weak to conster of the great.
Why not? although we are but born of earth,
We may behold the heavens, despising death;
And loving heaven that is so far above,
May in the end vouchsafe us entire love.
Therefore sweet Memory do thou retain
Those pleasures past, which will not turn again;
Remember beauteous Dorset's former sports,
So far from being touched by ill reports;   120
Wherein my self did always bear a part,
While reverend love presented my true heart:
Those recreations let me bear in mind,
Which her sweet youth and noble thoughts did find:
Whereof deprived, I evermore must grieve,
Hating blind Fortune, careless to relieve.

And you sweet Cookham , whom these ladies leave,
I now must tell the grief you did conceive
At their departure; when they went away,
How everything retained a sad dismay: 130
Nay long before, when once an inkling came,
Me thought each thing did unto sorrow frame:
The trees that were so glorious in our view,
Forsook both flow'rs and fruit, when once they knew
Of your depart, their very leaves did wither,
Changing their colours as they grew together.
But when they saw this had no pow'r to stay you,
They often wept, though, speechless, could not pray you;
Letting their tears in your fair bosoms fall,
As if they said, Why will ye leave us all?   140
This being vain, they cast their leaves away,
Hoping that pity would have made you stay:
Their frozen tops, like age's hoary hairs,
Shows their disasters, languishing in fears:
A swarthy rivelled rind all over spread,
Their dying bodies half alive, half dead.
But your occasions called you so away,
That nothing there had pow'r to make you stay:
Yet did I see, a noble grateful mind,
Requiting each according to their kind,   150
Forgetting not to turn and take your leave
Of these sad creatures, pow'rless to receive
Your favour, when with grief you did depart,
Placing their former pleasures in your heart;
Giving great charge to noble Memory,
There to preserve their love continually:
But specially the love of that fair tree,
That first and last you did vouchsafe to see:
In which it pleased you oft to take the air,
With noble Dorset, then a virgin fair: 160
Where many a learned book was read and scanned.
To this fair tree, taking me by the hand,
You did repeat the pleasures which had passed,

Seeming to grieve they could no longer last.
And with a chaste, yet loving kiss took leave,
Of which sweet kiss I did it soon bereave:
Scorning a senseless creature should possess
So rare a favour, so great happiness.
No other kiss it could receive from me,
For fear to give back what it took of thee: 170
So I ingrateful creature did deceive it,
Of that which you vouchsafed in love to leave it.
And that it oft had giv'n me much content,
Yet this great wrong I never could repent:
But of the happiest made it most forlorn,
To show that nothing's free from Fortune's scorn,
While all the rest with this most beauteous tree,
Made their sad concert sorrow's harmony.
The flow'rs that on the banks and walls did grow,
Crept in the ground, the grass did weep for woe.   180
The winds and waters seem to chide together
Because you went away they knew not whither:
And those sweet brooks that ran so fair and clear,
With grief and trouble wrinkled did appear.
Those pretty birds that wonted were to sing,
Now neither sing nor chirp, nor use their wing;
But with their tender feet on some bare spray,
Warble forth sorrow, and their own dismay.
Fair Philomela leaves her mournful ditty,
Drowned in dead sleep, yet can procure no pity: 190
Each arbour, bank, each seat, each stately tree,
Looks bare and desolate for want of thee;
Turning green tresses into frosty gray,
While in cold grief they wither all away.
The sun grew weak, his beams no comfort gave,
While all green things did make the earth their grave:
Each briar, each bramble, when you went away,
Caught fast your clothes, thinking to make you stay:
Delightful Echo wonted to reply
To our last words, did now for sorrow die: 200

The house cast off each garment that might grace it,
Putting on dust and cobwebs to deface it.
All desolation then there did appear,
When you were going whom they held so dear.
This last farewell to Cookham here I give,
When I am dead thy name in this may live,
Wherein I have performed her noble hest,
Whose virtues lodge in my unworthy breast,
And ever shall, so long as life remains,
Tying my heart to her by those rich chains.   210

LADY MARY WROTH
1587?-1652?

> Then if with grief I now must coupled be,
> Sorrow I'll wed: Despair thus governs me

Niece of Lady Mary Herbert and of Sir Philip Sidney, and eldest daughter of Lady Barbara (Gamage) and Sir Robert Sidney. In 1603 was, as Ben Jonson later put it, 'unworthily married to a jealous husband', Sir Robert Wroth, who did not share her interests (the only book dedicated to him was *A treatise on Madde Dogges*). He died in 1614, leaving her a month-old son and considerable debts; on the son's death in 1616 she lost the estate, and thereafter suffered financial difficulties. She became scandalous for her relationship (perhaps before 1614) with her first cousin, William Herbert, Earl of Pembroke, and bore him two illegitimate children. In 1621 published under her own name (equally scandalously) a romance (the first by a woman), *The Countess of Montgomerie's Urania*, with a sonnet-sequence, *Pamphilia to Amphilanthus*: the mode is Petrarchan, the love clandestine, the themes, constancy, frustration and insecurity, the atmosphere claustrophobic. In this selection, punctuation also has been modernized.

Josephine A. Roberts (ed), *The Poems of Lady Mary Wroth* (Baton Rouge and London: Louisiana State UP, 1983).

Sonnets from *Pamphilia to Amphilanthus*

9

Led by the pow'r of grief, to wailings brought
  By false conceit of change fall'n on my part,
  I seek for some small ease by lines which, bought,
  Increase the pain; grief is not cured by art:

Ah! how unkindness moves within the heart
  Which still is true, and free from changing thought;
  What unknown woe it breeds, what endless smart
  With ceaseless tears, which causelessly are wrought.

It makes me now to shun all shining light,
   And seek for blackest clouds me light to give,   **10**
   Which to all others, only darkness drive:
   They on me shine, for sun disdains my sight.

Yet though I dark do live, I triumph may;
Unkindness nor this wrong shall love allay.

24

When last I saw thee, I did not thee see,
   It was thine image, which in my thoughts lay
   So lively figured, as no time's delay
   Could suffer me in heart to parted be;

And sleep so favourable is to me,
   As not let thy loved remembrance stray,
   Lest that I, waking, might have cause to say
   There was one minute found to forget thee;

Then since my faith is such, so kind my sleep
   That gladly thee presents into my thought: **10**
   And still true-lover-like, thy face doth keep,
   So as some pleasure shadow-like is wrought.

Pity my loving, nay, of conscience give
Reward to me in whom thy self doth live.

39

Take heed mine eyes, how you your looks do cast,
   Lest they betray my heart's most secret thought;
   Be true unto your selves, for nothing's bought
   More dear than doubt, which brings a lover's fast.

Catch you all watching eyes ere they be past,
   Or take yours, fixed where your best love hath sought
   The pride of your desires; let them be taught
   Their faults, for shame they could no truer last.

Then look, and look with joy, for conquest won
   Of those that searched your hurt in double kind;   10
   So you kept safe, let them themselves look blind,
   Watch, gaze, and mark, till they to madness run;

While you, mine eyes, enjoy full sight of love,
Contented that such happinesses move.

40

False hope, which feeds but to destroy, and spill
   What it first breeds; unnatural to the birth
   Of thine own womb; conceiving but to kill,
   And plenty gives to make the greater dearth;

So tyrants do who, falsely ruling earth,
   Outwardly grace them, and with profit's fill
   Advance those, who appointed are to death,
   To make their greater fall to please their will.

Thus shadow they their wicked vile intent,
   Colouring evil with a show of good,   10
While in fair shows their malice so is spent;
   Hope kills the heart, and tyrants shed the blood.

For hope deluding brings us to the pride
Of our desires, the farther down to slide.

68*
My pain, still smothered in my grieved breast,
   Seeks for some ease, yet cannot passage find

To be discharged of this unwelcome guest;
When most I strive, more fast his burdens bind:

Like to a ship on Goodwins cast by wind,
    The more she strives, more deep in sand is pressed
    Till she be lost; so am I, in this kind,
    Sunk, and devoured, and swallowed by unrest,

Lost, shipwrecked, spoiled, debarred of smallest hope,
    Nothing of pleasure left; save thoughts have scope   10
    Which wander may: Go then, my thoughts, and cry

Hope's perished; Love tempest-beaten; Joy lost.
    Killing despair hath all these blessings crossed,
    Yet faith still cries, Love will not falsify.

101

No time, no room, no thought, or writing can
    Give rest, or quiet to my loving heart,
    Nor can my memory or fancy scan
    The measure of my still renewing smart,

Yet would I not, dear Love, thou should'st depart,
    But let my passions as they first began
    Rule, wound, and please; it is thy choicest art
    To give disquiet, which seems ease to man;

When all alone, I think upon thy pain,
    How thou dost travail our best selves to gain,   10
    Then hourly thy lessons I do learn,

Think on thy glory, which shall still ascend
    Until the world come to a final end,
    And then shall we thy lasting pow'r discern.

from *The Countess of Montgomery's Urania*

33

Loss, my molester, at last patient be,
  And satisfied with thy curst self, or move
  Thy mournful force thus oft on perjured love,
  To waste a life which lives by mischief's fee.

Who will behold true misery, view me,
  And find, what wit hath feigned, I fully prove:
  A heaven-like blessing changed, thrown from above
  Into despair, whose worst ill I do see,

Had I not happy been, I had not known
  So great a loss: a king deposed, feels most   10
  The torment of a throne-like want, when lost,
  And up must look to what late was his own.

Lucifer down cast, his loss doth grieve,
  My Paradise of joy gone, do I live?

45

Did I boast of liberty?
  'Twas an insolency vain:
I do only look on thee,
  And I captive am again.

ANNE BRADSTREET
1613?-1672

One of the best-known of all the English – or American – women poets
of the century. Born in Northamptonshire, the second child of Dorothy
(York) and Thomas Dudley, who later became prominent among Puritans
in Leicestershire; in 1628 married Simon Bradstreet; in 1630, the
Dudleys and Bradstreets joined the Puritan emigration, going to Salem
in Massachusetts. There Anne bore eight children, and wrote poetry on
a wide range of subjects, including lengthy works on Biblical and recent
English history, though it is her more personal and domestic verse for
which she is usually now regarded. In 1652 *The Tenth Muse lately sprung
up in America* was entered in the Stationers' Register, a revised edition
appearing in Boston in 1678. Simon later became governor of Salem
during the period of witchcraft persecutions.

John H. Ellis (ed), *The Works of Anne Bradstreet in Prose and Verse* (Chesterton,
Mass., 1867; facsimile reprint, Gloucester, Mass: Peter Smith,
1962); Elizabeth Wade White, *Anne Bradstreet: 'The Tenth Muse'* (NY: OUP,
1971).

*The Prologue**

To sing of wars, of captains, and of kings,
Of cities founded, commonwealths begun,
For my mean pen are too superior things:
Or how they all, or each their dates have run
Let poets and historians set these forth,
My obscure lines shall not so dim their worth.

But when my wondering eyes and envious heart
Great Bartas' sugared lines do but read o'er,
Fool I do grudge the Muses did not part
'Twixt him and me that overfluent store;   10
A Bartas can do what a Bartas will
But simple I according to my skill.

51

From schoolboy's tongue no rhet'ric we expect,
Nor yet a sweet consort from broken strings,
Nor perfect beauty where's a main defect:
My foolish, broken, blemished Muse so sings,
And to this mend, alas, no art is able,
'Cause nature made it so irreparable.

Nor can I, like that fluent sweet-tongued Greek,
Who lisped at first, in future times speak plain. 20
By art he gladly found what he did seek,
A full requital of his striving pain.
Art can do much, but this maxim's most sure:
A weak or wounded brain admits no cure.

I am obnoxious to each carping tongue
Who says my hand a needle better fits,
A poet's pen all scorn I thus should wrong,
For such despite they cast on female wits:
If what I do prove well, it won't advance,
They'll say it's stol'n, or else it was by chance. 30

But sure those antique Greeks were far more mild,
Else, of our sex why feigned they those nine,
And poesy made Calliope's own child;
So 'mongst the rest they placed the arts divine:
But this weak knot they will full soon untie,
The Greeks did naught but play the fool and lie.

Let Greeks be Greeks, and women what they are,
Men have precedency and still excel,
It is but vain unjustly to wage war;
Men can do best, and women know it well. 40
Pre-eminence in all and each is yours;
Yet grant some small acknowledgement of ours.

And oh ye high flown quills that soar the skies,
And ever with your prey still catch your praise,

If e'er you deign these lowly lines your eyes,
Give thyme or parsley wreath, I ask no bays;
This mean and unrefined ore of mine
Will make your glist'ring gold but more to shine.

To my Dear and loving Husband

If ever two were one, then surely we.
If ever man were loved by wife, then thee;
If ever wife was happy in a man,
Compare with me ye women if you can.
I prize thy love more than whole mines of gold,
Or all the riches that the East doth hold.
My love is such that rivers cannot quench,
Nor aught but love from thee, give recompence.
Thy love is such I can no way repay,
The heavens reward thee manifold I pray.   10
Then while we live, in love let's so persever,
That when we live no more, we may live ever.

Before the Birth of one of her Children

All things within this fading world hath end,
Adversity doth still our joys attend;
No ties so strong no friends so clear and sweet,
But with death's parting blow is sure to meet.
The sentence past is most irrecoverable,
A common thing, yet oh inevitable;
How soon, my Dear, death may my steps attend,
How soon't may be thy lot to lose thy friend,
We both are ignorant, yet love bids me
These farewell lines to recommend to thee,   10
That when that knot's untied that made us one,
I may seem thine, who in effect am none.
And if I see not half my days that's due

What nature would, God grant to yours and you;
The many faults that well you know I have,
Let be interred in my oblivious grave;
If any worth or virtue were in me,
Let that live freshly in thy memory,
And when thou feel'st no griefs, as I no harms,
Yet love thy dead, who long lay in thine arms: 20
And when thy loss shall be repaid with gains
Look to my little babes my dear remains.
And if thou love thy self, or loved'st me
These O protect from stepdame's injury.
And if chance to thine eyes shall bring this verse,
With some sad sighs honour my absent hearse;
And kiss this paper for thy love's dear sake,
Who with salt tears this last farewell did take.

A Letter to her Husband, absent upon Publick employment*

My head, my heart, mine eyes, my life, nay more,
My joy, my magazine of earthly store,
If two be one, as surely thou and I,
How stayest thou there, whilst I at Ipswich lie?
So many steps, head from the heart to sever;
If but a neck, soon should we be together:
I, like the earth this season, mourn in black,
My sun is gone so far in's zodiac,
When whilst I 'joyed, nor storms, nor frosts I felt,
His warmth such frigid colds did cause to melt.   10
My chilled limbs now numbed lie forlorn;
Return, return sweet Sol from Capricorn;
In this dead time, alas, what can I more
Than view those fruits which through thy heat I bore?
Which sweet contentment yield me for a space,
True living pictures of their father's face.

O strange effect! now thou art southward gone,
I weary grow, the tedious day so long;
But when thou northward to me shalt return,
I wish my sun may never set, but burn   20
Within the Cancer of my glowing breast,
The welcome house of him my dearest guest.
Where ever, ever stay, and go not thence,
Till nature's sad decree shall call thee hence;
Flesh of thy flesh, bone of thy bone,
I here, thou there, yet both but one.

Upon the Burning of our House July 10th 1666
Copied out of a loose paper

In silent night when rest I took
For sorrow near I did not look
I wakened was with thund'ring noise
And piteous shrieks of dreadful voice.
That fearful sound of 'Fire!' and 'Fire!'
Let no man know is my desire.
I, starting up, the light did spy,
And to my God my heart did cry
To strengthen me in my distress
And not to leave me succourless.   10
Then, coming out, beheld a space
The flame consume my dwelling place.
And when I could no longer look,
I blessed His name that gave and took,
That laid my goods now in the dust.
Yea, so it was, and so 'twas just.
It was His own, it was not mine,
Far be it that I should repine;
He might of all justly bereft
But yet sufficient for us left.   20
When by the ruins oft I passed

My sorrowing eyes aside did cast,
And here and there the places spy
Where oft I sat and long did lie:
Here stood that trunk, and there that chest,
There lay that store I counted best.
My pleasant things in ashes lie,
And them behold no more shall I.
Under thy roof no guest shall sit,
Nor at thy table eat a bit.   30
No pleasant tale shall e'er be told,
Nor things recounted done of old.
No candle e'er shall shine in thee,
Nor bridegroom's voice e'er heard shall be.
In silence ever shall thou lie,
Adieu, adieu, all's vanity.
Then straight I 'gin my heart to chide,
And did thy wealth on earth abide?
Did'st fix thy hope on mould'ring dust?
The arm of flesh didst make thy trust?   40
Raise up thy thoughts above the sky
That dunghill mists away may fly.
Thou hast an house on high erect,
Framed by that mighty Architect,
With glory richly furnished,
Stands permanent though this be fled.
It's purchased and paid for too
By Him who hath enough to do.
A price so vast as is unknown
Yet by His gift is made thine own;   50
There's wealth enough, I need no more,
Farewell, my pelf, farewell my store.
The world no longer let me love,
My hope and treasure lies above.

                                        A.B.

AN COLLINS
fl. 1653?

Nothing is known, and little can be deduced from her only book, except chronic illness – 'restrained from bodily employment' – and religious orthodoxy. The verse shows considerable technical experimentation and skill.

Divine Songs and Meditacions Composed By An Collins (London, 1653); reprinted in Stanley N. Stewart (ed.), (Augustan Reprint Society Pubs., San Marino, Calif., 1961).

Song

The winter being over,
   In order comes the spring,
Which doth green herbs discover,
   And cause the birds to sing.
The night also expired,
   Then comes the morning bright,
Which is so much desired
   By all that love the light.
     This may learn
     Them that mourn,   10
   To put their grief to flight:
The spring succeedeth winter,
   And day must follow night.

He therefore that sustaineth
   Affliction or distress,
Which every member paineth,
   And findeth no release:
Let such therefore despair not,
But on firm hope depend,
Whose griefs immortal are not,
   And therefore must have end.
     They that faint

With complaint
Therefore are to blame:
They add to their afflictions,
And amplify the same.

Another Song*

The winter of my infancy being over-past
I then supposed, suddenly the spring would haste
Which useth everything to cheer
With invitation to recreation
This time of year.

The sun sends forth his radiant beams to warm the ground,
The drops distil, between the gleams delights abound,
Ver brings her mate the flowery queen,
The groves she dresses, her art expresses
On ev'ry green.   10

But in my spring it was not so, but contrary,
For no delightful flowers grew to please the eye,
No hopeful bud, nor fruitful bough,
No mod'rate showers which causeth flowers
To spring and grow.

My April was exceeding dry, therefore unkind;
Whence 'tis that small utility I look to find,
For when that April is so dry
(As hath been spoken) it doth betoken
Much scarcity.   20

Thus is my spring now almost past in heaviness
The sky of my pleasure's over-cast with sad distress
For by a comfortless eclipse
Disconsolation and sore vexation,
My blossom nips.

Yet as a garden is my mind enclosed fast
Being to safety so confined from storm and blast
Apt to produce a fruit most rare,
That is not common with ev'ry woman
That fruitful are.   30

A love of goodness is the chiefest plant therein
The second is, (for to be brief) dislike to sin.
These grow in spite of misery,
Which Grace doth nourish and ease to flourish
Continually.

But evil motions, corrupt seeds, fall here also
Whence spring profaneness as do weeds where flowers grow
Which must supplanted be with speed
These weeds of error, distrust and terror,
Lest woe succeed.   40

So shall they not molest, the plants before expressed
Which countervails these outward wants, and purchase rest
Which more commodious is for me
Than outward pleasures or earthly treasures
Enjoyed would be.

My little hopes of worldly gain I fret not at,
As yet I do this hope retain; though spring be late
Perhaps my summer-age may be,
Not prejudicial, but beneficial
Enough for me.   50

Admit the worst, if it be not so, but stormy too,
I'll learn my self to undergo more than I do
And still content my self with this
Sweet meditation and contemplation
Of heav'nly bliss,

Which for the saints reserved is who persevere
In piety and holiness, and godly fear,
The pleasures of which bliss divine
Neither logician nor rhetorician
Can e'er define.   60

MARGARET CAVENDISH
DUCHESS OF NEWCASTLE
1624?-1674

'All I desire is Fame', she wrote in her first published volume. Eighth child of Sir Thomas Lucas of Colchester, who died in her infancy, and Elizabeth, daughter of John Leighton; patchily educated. After the outbreak of the Civil War went to Court as Maid of Honour to Queen Henrietta Maria, accompanying her into exile in Paris. There, in 1645, married William Cavendish, Marquis (later Duke) of Newcastle, minor poet and notable former commander in Charles's army, a widower of fifty-two looking for a young wife and more children; though childless, the marriage was happy. In 1653 published *Poems, and Fancies* and *Philosophicall Fancies*, claiming to have first expressed herself in verse because 'errours might better pass there than in Prose'. After the Restoration, the Cavendishes retired to his Welbeck Abbey estates; she wrote stories, plays, letters, philosophical and scientific speculations, and her husband's biography, but was better known as an eccentric. Pepys records seeing her in London in 1667, '...as I have often heard her described (for all the town talk is nowadays of her extravagancies), with her velvet cap, her hair about her ears, many black patches because of pimples about her mouth, naked necked, without anything about it, and a black juste-au-corps; she seemed to me a very comely woman'. Mary Evelyn found her manners and talk 'as airy, empty, whimsical, and rambling as her books', but Virginia Woolf wrote with passionate sympathy: 'What could bind, tame or civilise for human use that wild, generous, untutored intelligence?... What a vision of loneliness and riot the thought of Margaret Cavendish brings to mind! as if some great giant cucumber had spread itself over all the roses and carnations in the garden and choked them to death'.

Poems, and Fancies London, 1653, rev. ed., 1664; *Natures Pictures*, 1656; Virginia Woolf, *The Common Reader* (London: Hogarth Press, 1925); *A Room of One's Own* (London: Hogarth Press, 1929); Sara Heller Mendelson, *The Mental World of Stuart Women* (Brighton: Harvester, 1987); Kathleen Jones, *A Glorious Fame*, (London: Bloomsbury, 1988).

An Excuse for so much writ upon my Verses*

Condemn me not for making such a coil
About my book, alas it is my child.
Just like a bird, when her young are in nest,
Goes in, and out, and hops, and takes no rest;
But when their young are fledged, their heads out peep,
Lord what a chirping does the old one keep.
So I, for fear my strengthless child should fall
Against a door, or stool, aloud I call,
Bid have a care of such a dangerous place:
Thus write I much, to hinder all disgrace.   10

'A poet I am neither born, nor bred'

A Poet I am neither born, nor bred,
But to a witty poet married:
Whose brain is fresh, and pleasant, as the spring,
Where fancies grow, and where the Muses sing.
There oft I lean my head, and list'ning hark,
To hear his words, and all his fancies mark;
And from that garden flowers of fancies take,
Whereof a posy up in verse I make.
Thus I, that have no garden of mine own,
There gather flowers that are newly blown   10

Of the Theam of Love

O Love, how thou art tired out with rhyme!
Thou art a tree whereon all poets climb;
And from thy branches every one takes some
Of thy sweet fruit, which fancy feeds upon.
But now thy tree is left so bare, and poor,
That they can hardly gather one plum more.

62

Natures Cook*

Death is the cook of Nature; and we find
Meat dressed several ways to please her mind.
Some meats she roasts with fevers, burning hot,
And some she boils with dropsies in a pot.
Some for jelly consuming by degrees,
And some with ulcers, gravy out to squeeze.
Some flesh as sage she stuffs with gouts, and pains,
Others for tender meat hangs up in chains.
Some in the sea she pickles up to keep,
Others, as brawn is soused, those in wine steep.   10
Some with the pox, chops flesh, and bones so small,
Of which she makes a French fricasse withal.
Some on gridirons of calentures is broiled,
And some is trodden on, and so quite spoiled.
But those are baked, when smothered they do die,
By hectic fevers some meat she doth fry.
In sweat sometimes she stews with savoury smell,
A hodge-podge of diseases tasteth well.
Brains dressed with apoplexy to Nature's wish,
Or swims with sauce of megrims in a dish.   20
And tongues she dries with smoke from stomachs ill,
Which as the second course she sends up still.
Then Death cuts throats, for blood-puddings to make,
And puts them in the guts, which colics rack.
Some hunted are by Death, for deer that's red.
Or stall-fed oxen, knocked on the head.
Some for bacon by Death are singed, or scaled,
Then powdered up with phlegm, and rheum that's salt.

A Dissert*

Sweet marmalade of kisses new gathered,
Preserved children that are not fathered:
Sugar of beauty which melts away soon,

Marchpane of youth, and childish macaroon.
Sugar-plum words most sweet on the lips,
And wafer promises, which waste into chips.
Biscuit of love, which crumbles all away,
Jelly of fear, that quaking, quivering lay.
Then came in a fresh green-sickness cheese,
And tempting apples, like those eat by Eve;   10
With cream of honour, thick and good,
Firm nuts of friendship by it stood.
Grapes of delight, dull spirits to revive,
Whose juice, 'tis said, doth Nature keep alive.
Then Nature rose, when eat, and drank her fill,
To rest her self in ease, she's pleased with still.

Soule, and Body

Great Nature she doth clothe the soul within,
A fleshly garment which the Fates do spin.
And when these garments are grown old, and bare,
With sickness torn, Death takes them off with care.
And folds them up in peace, and quiet rest,
So lays them safe within an earthly chest.
Then scours them, and makes them sweet, and clean,
Fit for the soul to wear those clothes again.

A Woman drest by Age

A milk-white hair-lace wound up all her hairs,
And a deaf coif did cover both her ears,
A sober countenance about her face she ties,
And a dim sight doth cover half her eyes,
About her neck a kercher of coarse skin,
Which Time had crumpled, and worn creases in,
Her gown was turned to melancholy black,
Which loose did hang upon her sides and back,

Her stockings cramps had knit, red worsted gout,
And pains as garters tied her legs about.
A pair of palsy gloves her hands drew on,
With weakness stitched, and numbness trimmed upon.
Her shoes were corns, and hard skin sewed together,
Hard skin were soles, and corns the upper leather.
A mantle of diseases laps her round,
And thus she's dressed, till Death lays her in ground.

Of the Animal Spirits*

Those spirits which we Animal do call,
May men, and women be, and creatures small;
And in the body, kingdoms may divide,
As nerves, muscles, veins, and arteries wide.
The head, and heart, East and West Indies be,
Which through the veins may traffic, as the sea:
In fevers great by shipwreck many dies,
For when the blood is hot, and vapours rise
On boiling pulse, as waves they toss, if hit
Against hard rock of great obstructions, split.   10
Head the East Indies, where spicy fancy grows,
From oranges and lemons sharp satire flows;
The heart the West, where heat the blood refines,
Which blood is gold, and silver heart the mines.
Those from the head in ships their spice they fetch,
And from the heart the gold and silver rich.

A Dialogue betwixt the Body and the Mind

Body: What bodies else but Man's did Nature make,
        To join with such a mind, no rest can take;
        That ebbs, and flows, with full, and falling tide,
        As minds dejected fall, or swell with pride:
        In waves of passion roll to billows high,
        Always in motion, never quiet lie.

Where thoughts like fishes swim the mind about,
Where the grèat thoughts the smaller thoughts eat out.
My body the barque rows in mind's ocean wide,
Whose waves of passions beat on every side.   10
When that dark cloud of ignorance hangs low,
And winds of vain opinions strong do blow;
Then showers of doubts into the mind rain down,
In deep vast studies my barque of flesh is drowned.

Mind: Why doth the body thus complain, when I
Do help it forth of every misery?
For in the world your barque is bound to swim,
Nature hath rigged it out to traffic in.
Against hard rocks you break in pieces small,
If my invention help you not in all.   20
The lodestone of attraction I find out,
The card of observation guides about.
The needle of discretion points the way,
Which makes your barque get safe into each bay.

Body: If I 'scape drowning in the wat'ry main,
Yet in great mighty battles I am slain.
By your ambition I am forced to fight,
When many winds upon my body light.
For you care not, so you a fame may have,
To live, if I be buried in a grave.   30

Mind: If bodies fight, and kingdoms win, then you
Take all the pleasure that belongs thereto.
You have a crown, your head for to adorn,
Upon your body jewels are hung on.
All things are sought, to please your senses five,
No drug unpractised, to keep you alive.
And I, to set you up in high degree,
Invent all engines used in war to be.
'Tis I that make you in great triumph sit,
Above all other creatures high to get: 40
By the industrious arts, which I do find,
You other creatures in subjection bind:
You eat their flesh, and after that their skin,

66

When winter comes, you lap your bodies in.
And so of every thing that Nature makes,
By my direction you great pleasure takes.

Body: What though my senses all do take delight,
Yet you my entrails always bite.
My flesh eat up, that all my bones are bare,
With the sharp teeth of sorrow, grief and care.   50
Draws out my blood from veins, with envious spite,
Decays my strength with shame, or extreme fright.
With love extremely sick I lie,
With cruel hate you make me die.

Mind: Care keeps you from all hurt, or falling low,
Sorrow, and grief are debts to friends we owe.
Fear makes men just, to give each one his own,
Shame makes civility, without there's none.
Hate makes good laws, that all may live in peace,
Love brings society, and gets increase.   60
Besides, with joy I make the eyes look gay,
With pleasing smiles they dart forth everyway.
With mirth the cheeks are fat, smooth, rosy-red,
Your speech flares wit, when fancies fill the head.
If I were gone, you'd miss the company,
Wish we were joined again, or you might die.

from the battle episode in *The Fort or Castle of Hope**

Some with sharp swords, to tell O most accursed!
Were above half into their bodies thrust,
From whence fresh streams of blood along did run
Unto the hilts and there lay clodded on;
Some, their legs dangling by the nervous strings
And shoulders cut loose like flying wings;
Heads were cleft in pieces, brains lay mashed
And all their faces into slices hashed;
Brains only in the *pia-mater* thin
Did quivering lie within that little skin;   10

Their skulls, all broke and into pieces burst,
By horses' hoofs and chariot wheels crushed.
Others, their heads did lie on their own laps,
And some again, half cut, lay on their paps;
Some thrust their tongues out of their mouths at length,
For why, the strings were cut that gave them strength.
Their eyes did stare, their lids were open wide,
For the small nerves were shrunk on every side.
In some again those glassy balls hung by
Small slender strings, as chains, to tie the eye,   20
Which strings when broke, the eyes fell trundling round,
And then the film was broke upon the ground.
In death their teeth strong set, their lips were bare,
Which grinning seemed as if they angry were;
Their hair upon their eyes in clodded gore
So wildly spread as ne'er it did before;
With frowns their foreheads did in furrows lie
As graves, their foes to bury when they die.
Their spongy lungs, heaved up through pangs of death,
With pain and difficulty fetched short breath;   30
Some grasping hard their hands through pain provoked
Because the rattling phlegm their throats had choked.
Their bodies now bowed up, then down did fall
For want of strength to make them stand withal;
Some staggering on their legs did feebly stand,
Or leaning on their sword with either hand
Where on the pommel did their breast rely,
More grieved they could not fight than for to die [. . .]

A Discourse of Beasts

Who knows, but beasts, as they do lie,
In meadows low, or else on mountains high,
But that they do contemplate on the sun,
And how his daily, yearly circles run.
Whether the sun about the earth doth rove

Or else the earth upon its own poles move.
And in the night, when twinkling stars we see,
Like Man, imagines them all suns to be:
And may like Man, stars, planets number well,
And could they speak, they might their motions tell.   10
And how the planets in each orb do move:
'Gainst their astrology can no man prove.
For they may know the stars, and their aspects,
What influence they cast, and their effects.

KATHERINE PHILIPS
1631-1664

Dubbed by her admirers 'The Matchless Orinda', and usually compared favourably with Aphra Behn ('The Incomparable Astraea'), if only on grounds of morality and professed modesty (though she knew 'everybody'); 'very good-natured; not at all high-minded; pretty fatt; not tall; red pumpled face; wrote out Verses in Innes, or Mottos in windowes, in her table-booke', wrote Aubrey. The daughter of a successful London merchant, John Fowler, and his second wife, Katherine Oxenbridge, who herself remarried a Parliamentarian baronet, Sir Richard Philips, in 1646; in 1648 was married to James Philips, aged 54, a widower kinsman of her stepfather; bore two children. Despite her Puritan family, she had Royalist sympathies, and developed connections with Cavalier circles that after the Restoration, which ruined her husband, were (possibly literally) life-savers. Developed intense Platonic-romantic relationships with various young ladies, and a cult of friendship. Her translation of Corneille's *La Mort de Pompée* in 1663 made her reputation; four acts through translating his *Horace* she contracted small-pox, and died in London.

Poems, By the Most Deservedly Admired Mrs. Katherine Philips, The Matchless Orinda (London, 1667); G. Saintsbury (ed.), *The Caroline Poets*, Vol.I (Oxford: Clarendon, 1905); Philip Souers, *The Matchless Orinda* (Cambridge, Mass, 1931); Lillian Federman, *Surpassing the Love of Men: Romantic Friendship and Love Between Women from the Renaissance to the Present* (NY: William Morrow, 1981).

*Friendship's Mystery, to my dearest Lucasia**
I
Come, my Lucasia, since we see
    That miracles men's faith do move,
By wonder and by prodigy
    To the dull angry world let's prove
    There's a religion in our love.

70

II

For though we were designed t'agree,
　　That fate no liberty destroys,
But our election is as free
　　As angels', who with greedy choice
　　Are yet determined to their joys.　　　　　　　　**10**

III

Our hearts are doubled by the loss,
　　Here mixture is addition grown;
We both diffuse, and both ingross:
　　And we whose minds are so much one,
　　Never, yet ever are alone.

IV

We court our own captivity
　　Than thrones more great and innocent:
'Twere banishment to be set free,
　　Since we wear fetters whose intent
　　Not bondage is but ornament.　　　　　　　　**20**

V

Divided joys are tedious found,
　　And griefs united easier grow;
We are ourselves but by rebound,
　　And all our titles shuffled so,
　　Both princes, and both subjects too.

VI

Our hearts are mutual victims laid,
　　While they (such power in friendship lies)
Are altars, priests, and off'rings made:
　　And each heart which thus kindly dies,
　　Grows deathless by the sacrifice.　　　　　　　　**30**

To my Excellent Lucasia, on our Friendship

I did not live until this time
   Crowned my felicity,
When I could say without a crime,
   I am not thine, but thee.

This carcase breathed, and walked, and slept,
   So that the world believed
There was a soul the motions kept;
   But they were all deceived.

For as a watch by art is wound
   To motion, such was mine: 10
But never had Orinda found
   A soul till she found thine;

Which now inspires, cures and supplies,
   And guides my darkened breast:
For thou art all that I can prize,
   My joy, my life, my rest.

No bridegroom's nor crown-conqueror's mirth
   To mine compared can be:
They have but pieces of this earth,
   I've all the world in thee.   20

Then let our flames still light and shine,
   And no false fear control,
As innocent as our design,
   Immortal as our soul.

An Answer to another persuading a Lady to marriage

I

Forbear, bold youth, all's Heaven here,
    And what you do aver,
To others courtship may appear,
    'Tis sacrifice to her.

II

She is a public deity,
    And were't not very odd
She should depose herself to be
    A petty household god?

III

First make the sun in private shine,
    And bid the world adieu,   10
That so he may his beams confine
    In compliment to you.

IV

But if of that you do despair,
    Think how you did amiss,
To strive to fix her beams, which are
    More bright and large than his.

To the Queen of Inconstancy, Regina Collier, in Antwerp

I

Unworthy, since thou hast decreed
Thy love and honour both shall bleed,
My friendship could not choose to die
In better time or company.

What thou hast got by this exchange
Thou wilt perceive, when the revenge
Shall by those treacheries be made,
For which our faith thou hast betrayed.

III

When thy idolators shall be
True to themselves, and false to thee,   10
Thou'lt see that in heart-merchandise,
Value, not number, makes the price.

IV

Live, to that day, my innocence
Shall be my friendship's just defence:
For this is all the world can find,
While thou wert noble, I was kind.

V

The desp'rate game that thou dost play
At private ruins cannot stay:
The horrid treachery of that face
Will sure undo its native place.   20

VI

Then let the Frenchmen never fear
The victory while thou art there;
For if sins will call judgements down,
Thou hast enough to stock the town.

*Epitaph on her Son H.P.**
at St Syth's Church, where her body also lies interred

What on earth deserves our trust?
Youth and beauty both are dust.
Long we gathering are with pain,
What one moment calls again.

Seven years' childless marriage past,
A son, a son is born at last:
So exactly limbed and fair,
Full of good spirits, mien, and air,
As a long life promised,
Yet, in less than six weeks dead.   10
Too promising, too great a mind
In so small room to be confined:
Therefore, as fit in Heav'n to dwell,
He quickly broke the prison shell.
So the subtle alchemist
Can't with Hermes' seal resist
The powerful spirit's subtler flight,
But 'twill bid him long good night:
And so the sun, if it arise
Half so glorious as his eyes,   20
Like this infant, takes a shroud,
Buried in a morning cloud.

*Lucasia, Rosania and Orinda parting at a Fountain, July 1663**

I

Here, here are our enjoyments done,
    And since the love and grief we wear
    Forbids us either word or tear,
And art wants here expression,
See Nature furnish us with one.

II

The kind and mournful nymph which here
    Inhabits in her humble cells,
    No longer her own sorrow tells
Nor for it now concerned appears,
But for our parting sheds these tears.   10

III

Unless she may afflicted be,
   Lest we should doubt her innocence,
   Since she hath lost her best pretence
Unto a matchless purity;
Our love being clearer far than she.

IV

Cold as the streams that from her flow,
   Or (if her privater recess
   A greater coldness can express)
Then cold as those dark beds of snow
Our hearts are at this parting blow.   20

V

But Time, that has both wings and feet,
   Our suffering minutes being spent,
   Will visit us with new content;
And sure, if unkindness be so sweet
'Tis harder to forget than meet.

VI

Then though the sad adieu we say,
   Yet as the wine we hither bring
   Revives, and then exalts the spring;
So let our hopes to meet allay
The fears and sorrows of this day.   30

APHRA BEHN
1640-1689

Little is certain about her early years: possibly the daughter of Bartholo-
mew and Elizabeth Johnson of Kent; in her youth probably went to
Surinam, where her (foster?) father had been given a colonial post but
died *en route*. While there, was involved with a slave rising (see her
prose romance *Oroonoko*, 1688); returning to England presumably mar-
ried a (Dutch?) tradesman who soon died. In 1666, was sent as a spy to
Holland; was not paid adequately, returned to London, and was briefly
imprisoned for debt. In 1670 began her career as the first professional
woman writer, producing some sixteen plays (notably *The Forc'd Marriage*
and *The Rover*) in nineteen years. Royalist, pro-Catholic, libertine, her
acquaintance ranged from the Earl of Rochester to Nell Gwynne. A vicious
lampoon survives from her declining years:

> Doth that lewd harlot, that poetic queen
> Fam'd through Whitefriars, you know who I mean,
> Mend for reproof, others set up in spight
> To flux, take glisters, vomits, purge and write.
> Long with a sciatica, she's beside lame,
> Her limbs distortur'd, nerves shrunk up with pain,
> And therefore I'll all sharp reflections shun,
> Poverty, poetry, pox, are plagues enough for one.

Perhaps surprisingly, is buried in Westminster Abbey, under a stone
reading, 'Here lies a Proof that wit can never be / Defence enough against
Mortality'.

Poems upon several occasions, with a voyage to the island of Love (London,
1684); *Lycidus, or the Lover in Fashion... Poems by Several Hands* (London,
1688); Montague Summers (ed.), *The Works of Aphra Behn* (London:
Heinemann, 1915); Maureen Duffy, *The Passionate Shepherdess: Aphra Behn
1640-1689* (London: Jonathan Cape, 1977).

Love Arm'd

Love in fantastic triumph sat,
Whilst bleeding hearts around him flowed,
For whom fresh pains he did create,

And strange tyrannic power he showed;
From thy bright eyes he took his fire,
Which round about, in sport he hurled;
But 'twas from mine, he took desire,
Enough to undo the amorous world.

From me he took his sighs and tears,
From thee his pride and cruelty;   10
From me his languishments and fears,
And every killing dart from thee;
Thus thou and I, the god have armed,
And set him up a deity;
But my poor heart alone is harmed,
Whilst thine the victor is, and free.

Song: The Willing Mistriss

Amyntas led me to a grove
    Where all the trees did shade us;
The sun it self, though it had strove,
    It could not have betrayed us:
The place secured from human eyes,
    No other fear allows,
But when the winds that gently rise,
    Does kiss the yielding boughs.

Down there we sat upon the moss,
    And did begin to play   10
A thousand amorous tricks, to pass
    The heat of all the day.
A many kisses he did give;
    And I returned the same
Which made me willing to receive
    That which I dare not name.

78

His charming eyes no aid required
   To tell their soft'ning tale;
On her that was already fired
   'Twas easy to prevail.   20
He did but kiss and clasp me round,
   Whilst those his thoughts expressed:
   And laid me gently on the ground;
   Ah who can guess the rest?

The Disappointment*

I

One day the amorous Lysander
By an impatient passion swayed,
Surprised fair Cloris, that loved maid,
Who could defend herself no longer.
All things did with his love conspire;
The gilded planet of the day,
In his gay chariot drawn by fire,
Was now descending to the sea,
And left no light to guide the world,
But what from Cloris' brighter eyes was hurled.   10

II

In a lone thicket made for love,
Silent as a yielding maid's consent,
She with a charming languishment,
Permits his force, yet gently strove;
Her hands his bosom softly meet,
But not to put him back designed,
Rather to draw him on inclined:
Whilst he lay trembling at her feet,
Resistance 'tis in vain to show;
She wants the power to say – Ah! What d'ye do?   20

III

Her bright eyes sweet, and yet severe,
Where love and shame confus'dly strive,
Fresh vigour to Lysander give;
And breathing faintly in his ear,
She cried – Cease, cease your vain desire,
Or I'll call out – What would you do?
My dearer honour ev'n to you
I cannot, must not give – Retire
Or take this life, whose chiefest part
I gave you with the conquest of my heart.   30

IV

But he as much unused to fear,
As he was capable of love,
The blessed minutes to improve,
Kisses her mouth, her neck, her hair;
Each touch her new desire alarms,
His burning trembling hand he pressed
Upon her swelling snowy breast,
While she lay panting in his arms.
All her unguarded beauties lie
The spoils and trophies of the enemy.   40

V

And now without respect or fear,
He seeks the object of his vows,
(His love no modesty allows)
By swift degrees advancing – where
His daring hand that altar seized,
Where gods of love do sacrifice:
That awful throne, that paradise
Where rage is calmed, and anger pleased;
That fountain where delight still flows,
And gives the universal world repose.   50

VI

Her balmy lips encount'ring his,
Their bodies, as their souls, are joined;
Where both in transports unconfined
Extend themselves upon the moss.
Cloris half dead and breathless lay;
Her soft eyes cast a humid light,
Such as divides the day and night;
Or falling stars, whose fires decay:
And now no signs of life she shows,
But what in short-breathed sighs returns and goes.   60

VII

He saw how at her length she lay;
He saw her rising bosom bare;
Her loose thin robes, through which appear
A shape designed for love and play;
Abandoned by her pride and shame.
She does her softest joys dispense,
Off'ring her virgin-innocence
A victim to love's sacred flame;
While the o'er-ravished shepherd lies
Unable to perform the sacrifice.   70

VIII

Ready to taste a thousand joys,
The too transported hapless swain
Found the vast pleasure turned to pain;
Pleasure which too much love destroys:
The willing garments by he laid,
And heaven all opened to his view,
Mad to possess, himself he threw
On the defenceless lovely maid.
But Oh what envying gods conspire
To snatch his power, yet leave him the desire!   80

81

IX

Nature's support (without whose aid
She can no humane being give)
It self now wants the art to live:
Faintness its slackened nerves invade:
In vain th'enraged youth essayed
To call its fleeting vigour back,
No motion 'twill from motion take;
Excess of love his love betrayed:
In vain he toils, in vain commands;
The insensible fell weeping in his hand.   90

X

In this so amorous cruel strife,
Where Love and Fate were too severe,
The poor Lysander in despair
Renounced his reason with his life:
Now all the brisk and active fire
That should the nobler part inflame,
Served to increase his rage and shame,
And left no spark for new desire:
Not all her naked charms could move
Or calm that rage that had debauched his love.   100

XI

Cloris returning from the trance
Which love and soft desire had bred,
Her timorous hand she gently laid
(Or guided by design or chance)
Upon that fabulous Priapas,
That potent god, as poets feign;
But never did young shepherdess,
Gath'ring of fern upon the plain,
More nimbly draw her fingers back,
Finding beneath the verdant leaves a snake: 110

XII

Than Cloris her fair hand withdrew,
Finding that god of her desires
Disarmed of all his awful fires,
And cold as flow'rs bathed in the morning dew.
Who can the nymph's confusion guess?
The blood forsook the hinder place,
And strewed with blushes all her face,
Which both disdain and shame expressed:
And from Lysander's arms she fled,
Leaving him fainting on that gloomy bed.   120

XIII

Like lightning through the grove she flies,
Or Daphne from the Delphic god,
No print upon the grassy road
She leaves, t'instruct pursuing eyes.
The wind that wantoned in her hair,
And with her ruffled garments played,
Discovered in the flying maid
All that the gods e'er made, if fair.
So Venus, when her love was slain,
With fear and haste flew o'er the fatal plain.   130

XIV

The nymph's resentments none but I
Can well imagine or condole:
But none can guess Lysander's soul,
But those who swayed his destiny.
His silent griefs swell up to storms,
And not one god his fury spares;
He cursed his birth, his fate, his stars;
But more the shepherdess's charms,
Whose soft bewitching influence
Had damned him to the hell of impotence.   140

To Alexis in Answer to his Poem against Fruition*

Ah hapless sex! who bear no charms,
But what like lightning flash and are no more,
 False fires sent down for baneful harms,
Fires which the fleeting lover feebly warms
 And given like past beboches o'er,
 Like songs that please, (though bad,) when new,
 But learned by heart neglected grew.

In vain did Heav'n adorn the shape and face
With beauties which by angels' forms it drew:
In vain the mind with brighter glories grace,   10
While all our joys are stinted to the space
 Of one betraying interview,
With one surrender to the eager will
We're short-lived nothing, or a real ill.

Since Man with that inconstancy was born,
To love the absent, and the present scorn,
 Why do we deck, why do we dress
 For such a short-lived happiness?
 Why do we put attraction on,
Since either way 'tis we must be undone?   20

 They fly if Honour take our part,
 Our virtue drives them o'er the field.
 We lose 'em by too much desert,
 And Oh! they fly us if we yield.
Ye Gods! is there no charm in all the fair
To fix this wild, this faithless wanderer.

 Man! our great business and our aim.
 For whom we spread our fruitless snares,
No sooner kindles the designing flame,
 But to the next bright object bears   30
The trophies of his conquest and our shame:
 Inconstancy's the god supreme
The rest is airy notion, empty dream!

84

Then, heedless nymph, be ruled by me
If e'er your swain the bliss desire;
   Think like Alexis he may be
   Whose wished possession damps his fire;
   The roving youth in every shade
Has left some sighing and abandoned maid,
For 'tis a fatal lesson he has learned,   40
After fruition ne'er to be concerned.

*To the fair Clarinda, who made Love to me, imagin'd more than Woman**

Fair lovely maid, or if that title be
Too weak, too feminine for nobler thee,
Permit a name that more approaches truth:
And let me call thee, lovely charming youth.
This last will justify my soft complaint;
While that may serve to lessen my constraint;
And without blushes I the youth pursue,
When so much beauteous woman is in view.
Against thy charms we struggle but in vain:
With thy deluding form thou giv'st us pain,   10
While the bright nymph betrays us to the swain.
In pity to our sex sure thou wert sent,
That we might love, and yet be innocent:
For sure no crime with thee we can commit;
Or if we should – thy form excuses it.
For who, that gathers fairest flowers believes
A snake lies hid beneath the fragrant leaves.

Thou beauteous wonder of a different kind,
Soft Cloris with the dear Alexis joined;
When e'er the manly part of thee would plead,   20
Thou tempts us with the image of the maid.
While we the noblest passions do extend
   The love to Hermes, Aphrodite the friend.

LADY MARY CHUDLEIGH
1656-1710

Father, Richard Lee, of Winslade, Devon; in 1674 married Sir George Chudleigh, of Ashton, Devon, and had three children. Widely read in classical and English literature, and an admirer of the feminist writer Mary Astell. Her verse is very assured and polished, high-minded and judgemental, celebrating female friendships and severe on husbands. *The Ladies Defence* was a response to a sermon by a Nonconformist minister, Mr Sprint, printed in 1699, about women's weak moral nature and need for absolute obedience to their husbands: it is for four speakers, Sir John Brute, a stupid, tyrannical husband, a Parson, not unrelated to Mr Sprint, Sir William Loveall, dim and chivalrous, and one Melissa, who has a few sharp things to say.

The Ladies Defence or, The Bride-Woman's Counsellor Answer'd: a poem (London, 1701); *Poems on Several Occasions* (London, 1710).

from *The Ladies Defence*
Or, the Bride-Woman's Counsellor Answered

Melissa: Unhappy they, who by their duty led,
Are made the partners of a hated bed;
And by their father's avarice or pride,
To empty fops, or nauseous clowns are tied;
Or else constrained to give up all their charms
Into an old ill-humoured husband's arms,
Who hugs his bags, and never was inclined
To be to aught besides his money kind,
Who's always positive in what is ill,
And still a slave to his imperious will: 10
Averse to any thing he thinks will please,
Still sick, and still in love with his disease:
With fears, with discontent, with envy curst,
To all uneasy, and himself the worst:
A spiteful censor of the present age,
Or dully jesting, or deformed with rage [. . .]

'Tis hard we should be by the men despised,
Yet kept from knowing what would make us prized:
Debarred from knowledge, banished from the schools,
And with the utmost industry bred fools.   20
Laughed out of reason, jested out of sense,
And nothing left but native innocence:
Then told we are incapable of wit,
And only for the meanest drudgeries fit:
Made slaves to serve their luxury and pride,
And with innumerable hardships tried,
Till pitying Heav'n release us from our pain [. . .]
  They think, if we our thoughts can but express,
And know but how to work, to dance and dress,
It is enough, as much as we should mind,   30
As if we were for nothing else designed,
But made, like puppets, to divert mankind.
O that my sex would all such toys despise;
And only study to be good, and wise [. . .]
  Through all the labyrinth of learning go,
And grow more humble, as they more do know.
By doing this, they will respect procure,
Silence the men, and lasting fame secure;
And to themselves the best companions prove,
And neither fear their malice, nor desire their love.   40

To the Ladies

Wife and servant are the same,
But only differ in the name:
For when that fatal knot is tied,
When she the word *Obey* has said,
And man by law supreme has made,
Then all that's kind is laid aside,
And nothing left but state and pride.
Fierce as an eastern prince he grows,
And all his innate rigour shows: 10

Then but to look, to laugh, or speak,
Will the nuptial contract break.
Like mutes, she signs alone must make,
And never any freedom take.
But still be governed by a nod,
And fear her husband as her god:
Him still must serve, him still obey,
And nothing act, and nothing say,
But what her haughty lord thinks fit
Who, with the power, has all the wit.   20
Then shun, oh! shun that wretched state,
And all the fawning flatt'rers hate.
Value yourselves, and men despise:
You must be proud, if you'll be wise.

Her identity is not known – nor even how much that is attributed to her is by the one person (for instance, 'To Bajazet' is of uncertain attribution). She expresses admiration for Aphra Behn, and her 'set' was clearly linked with the 'beau monde'. From the volume can be constructed the story of a protracted affair with a rakish older man, J.G., who jilted her and married abroad; her jealousy; her division between two men, and being jilted again.

Female Poems on Several Occasions (London, 1679, 1682).

On a Bashful Shepherd

I

Young Clovis by a happy chance,
His loved Ephelia spied,
In such a place, as might advance
His courage, and abate her pride:
With eyes that might have told his suit,
Although his bashful tongue was mute,
Upon her gazed he,
But the coy nymph, though in surprise,
Upon the ground fixing her eyes,
The language would not see.   10

II

With gentle grasps he wooed her hand,
And sighed in seeming pain,
But this she would not understand,
His sighs were all in vain:
Then change of blushes next he tried,
And gave his hand freedom to slide
Upon her panting breast;
Finding she did not this control,
Unto her lips he gently stole,
And bid her guess the rest.   20

III

She blushed, and turned her head aside,
And so much anger feigned,
That the poor shepherd almost died,
And she no breath retained:
Her killing frown so chilled his blood,
He like a senseless statue stood,
Nor further durst he woo,
And though his blessing was so near,
Checked by his modesty and fear,
He faintly let it go.   30

To One that asked me why I loved J.G.

Why do I love? go, ask the glorious sun
Why every day it round the earth doth run:
Ask Thames and Tiber why they ebb and flow:
Ask damask roses why in June they blow:
Ask ice and hail the reason why they're cold:
Decaying beauties, why they will grow old:
They'll tell thee, Fate, that everything doth move,
Enforces them to this, and me to love.
There is no reason for our love or hate,
'Tis irresistible as death or fate;   10
'Tis not his face; I've sense enough to see,
That is not good, though doted on by me:
Nor is't his tongue that has this conquest won,
For that at least is equalled by my own:
His carriage can to none obliging be,
'Tis rude, affected, full of vanity:
Strangely ill natured, peevish and unkind,
Unconstant, false, to jealousy inclined:
His temper could not have so great a power,
'Tis mutable, and changes every hour: 20
Those vigorous years that women so adore
Are past in him: he's twice my age and more;

And yet I love this false, this worthless man,
With all the passion that a woman can;
Dote on his imperfections, though I spy
Nothing to love; I love, and know not why.
Since 'tis decreed in the dark book of Fate,
That I should love, and he should be ingrate.

Maidenhead
Written at the request of a friend

At your entreaty, I at last have writ
This whimsy, that has nigh nonplussed my wit:
The toy I've long enjoyed, if it may
Be called t'enjoy, a thing we wish away;
But yet no more its character can give,
Than tell the minutes that I have to live:
'Tis a fantastic ill, a loathed disease,
That can no sex, no age, no person please:
Men strive to gain it, but the way they choose
T'obtain their wish, that and the wish doth lose;   10
Our thoughts are still uneasy, till we know
What 'tis, and why it is desired so:
But th'first unhappy knowledge that we boast,
Is that we know, the valued trifle's lost:
Thou dull companion of our active years,
That chill'st our warm blood with thy frozen fears:
How is it likely thou should'st long endure,
When thought it self the ruin may procure?
The short-lived tyrant, that usurp'st a sway
O'er woman-kind, though none thy pow'r obey,   20
Except th'ill-natured, ugly, peevish, proud,
And these indeed, thy praises sing aloud:
But what's the reason they obey so well?
Because they want the power to rebel:
But I forget, or have my subject lost:
Alas! thy being's fancy at the most:

Though much desired, 'tis but seldom men
Court the vain blessing from a woman's pen.

To a Proud Beauty*

Imperious fool! think not because you're fair,
That you so much above my converse are,
What though the gallants sing your praises loud,
And with false plaudits make you vainly proud?
Though they may tell you all adore your eyes,
And every heart's your willing sacrifice;
Or spin the flatt'ry finer, and persuade
Your easy vanity, that we were made
For foils to make your lustre shine more bright,
And must pay homage to your dazzling light,   10
Yet know whatever stories they may tell,
All you can boast, is, to be pretty well;
Know too, you stately piece of vanity,
That you are not alone adored, for I
Fantastically might mince, and smile, as well
As you, if airy praise my mind could swell:
Nor are the loud applauses that I have,
For a fine face, or things that Nature gave;
But for acquired parts, a gen'rous mind,
A pleasing converse, neither nice nor kind: 20
When they that strive to praise you most, can say
No more, but that you're handsome, brisk and gay:
Since then my frame's as great as yours is, why
Should you behold me with a loathing eye?
If you at me cast a disdainful eye,
In biting satire I will rage so high,
Thunder shall pleasant be to what I'll write,
And you shall tremble at my very sight;
Warned by your danger, none shall dare again
Provoke my pen to write in such a strain.   30

In the Person of a Lady, to Bajazet,
Her Unconstant Gallant*

How far are they deceived, that hope in vain
A lasting lease of joys from love t'obtain?
All the dear sweets we're promised, or expect,
After enjoyment turn to cold neglect:
Could love a constant happiness have known,
That mighty wonder had in me been shown;
Our passions were so favoured by Fate,
As if she meant them an eternal date:
So kind he looked, such tender words he spoke,
'Twas past belief such vows should e'er be broke: 10
Fixed on my eyes, how often would he say
He could with pleasure gaze an age away.
When thought too great for words, had made him mute,
In kisses he would tell my hand his suit:
So strong his passion was, so far above
The common gallantries that pass for love:
At worst, I thought, if he unkind should prove,
His ebbing passion would be kinder far,
Than the first transports of all others are: 20
Nor was my love weaker, or less than his;
In him I centered all my hopes of bliss:
For him, my duty to my friends forgot;
For him I lost – alas! what lost I not?
Fame, all the valuable things of life,
To meet his love by a less name than wife.
How happy was I then! how dearly blest!
When this great man lay panting on my breast,
Looking such things as ne'er can be expressed.
Thousand fresh loves he gave me every hour,   30
While eagerly I did his looks devour:
Quite overcome with charms, I trembling lay,
At every look he gave, melted away;
I was so highly happy in his love,
Methought I pitied those that dwell above.

Think then, thou greatest, loveliest, falsest man,
How you have vowed, how I have loved, and then
My faithless dear, be cruel if you can.
How I have loved I cannot, need not tell;
No, every act has shown I loved too well.   40
Since first I saw you, I ne'er had a thought
Was not entirely yours; to you I brought
My virgin innocence, and freely made
My love an offering to your noble bed:
Since when, you've been the star by which I've steered,
And nothing else but you, I've loved, or feared:
Your smiles I only lived by: and I must
When e'er you frown, be shattered into dust.
I cannot live on pity, or respect,
A thought so mean, would my whole frame infect,   50
Less than your love I scorn, sir, to accept.
Let me not live in dull indiff'rency,
But give me rage enough to make me die:
For if from you I needs must meet my fate,
Before your pity, I would choose your hate.

ANNE KILLIGREW
1660-1685

Daughter of Judith and Dr Henry Killigrew, chaplain to the Duke of York; the dramatists Thomas and Sir William Killigrew were her uncles; Maid of Honour to Mary of Modena, and rather ostentatiously virtuous, though charming in her naïveté. Died of small-pox; *Poems* appeared in 1685, though dated 1686, with an eulogistic poem by Dryden ('Thy father was transfus'd into thy blood: / So wert thou born into the tuneful strain...').

Poems by Mrs. Anne Killigrew, 1686. Reprinted in facsimile by Richard Morton, intro. and ed., Gainesville, Fla.)

On a picture Painted by her self, representing two Nimphs of Diana's, one in a Posture to Hunt, the other Batheing*

We are Diana's virgin-train,
Descended of no mortal strain;
Our bows and arrows are our goods,
Our palaces, the lofty woods,
The hills and dales, at early morn,
Resound and echo with our horn;
We chase the hind and fallow-deer,
The wolf and boar both dread our spear;
In swiftness we outstrip the wind,
An eye and thought we leave behind;   10
We fawns and shaggy satyrs awe;
To sylvan pow'rs we give the law:
Whatever does provoke our hate,
Our javelins strike, as sure as fate;
We bathe in springs, to cleanse the soil
Contracted by our eager toil,
In which we shine like glittering beams,
Or crystal in the crystal streams;
Though Venus we transcend in form,
No wanton flames our bosoms warm!   20
If you ask where such wights do dwell,

In what blest clime, that so excel?
The poets only that can tell.

On Death

Tell me thou safest end of all our woe,
Why wretched mortals do avoid thee so:
Thou gentle drier o'th' afflicted's tears,
Thou noble ender of the coward's fears;
Thou sweet repose to lovers' sad despair,
Thou calm t'ambition's rough tempestuous care.
If in regard of bliss thou wert a curse,
And than the joys of Paradise art worse;
Yet after man from his first station fell,
And God from Eden Adam did expel,   10
Thou wert no more an evil, but relief;
The balm and cure to ev'ry human grief:
Through thee, what man had forfeited before
He now enjoys, and ne'er can lose it more.
No subtle serpents in the grave betray,
Worms on the body there, not souls, do prey;
No vice there tempts, no terrors there affright,
No coz'ning sin affords a false delight:
No vain contentions do that peace annoy,
No fierce alarms break the lasting day.   20

Ah since from thee so many blessings flow,
Such real good as life can never know;
Come when thou wilt, in thy affrighting'st dress,
Thy shape shall never make thy welcome less.
Thou may'st to joy, but ne'er to fear give birth,
Thou best, as well as certain'st thing on earth.
Fly thee? May travellers then fly their rest,
And hungry infants fly the proffered breast.
No, those that faint and tremble at thy name,
Fly from their good on a mistaken fame.   30

Thus childish fear did Israel of old
From plenty and the Promised Land with-hold;
They fancied giants, and refused to go
When Canaan did with milk and honey flow.

Upon the saying that my verses were made by another*

Next Heaven my vows to thee (O sacred Muse!)
I offered up, nor didst thou them refuse.
    O Queen of Verse, said I, if thou'lt inspire,
And warm my soul with thy poetic fire,
No love of gold shall share with thee my heart,
Or yet ambition in my breast have part,
More rich, more noble I will ever hold
The Muses' laurel, than a crown of gold.
An undivided sacrifice I'll lay
Upon thine altar, soul and body pay;   10
Thou shalt my pleasure, my employment be,
And all I'll make a holocaust to thee.

    The deity that ever does attend
Prayers so sincere, to mine did condescend.
I writ, and the judicious praised my pen:
Could any doubt ensuing glory then?
What pleasing raptures filled my ravished sense?
How strong, how sweet, Fame, was thy influence?
And thine, False Hope, that to my flattered sight
Didst glories represent so near, and bright?   20
By thee deceived, methought each verdant tree
Apollo's transformed Daphne seemed to be;
And ev'ry fresher branch, and ev'ry bough
Appeared as garlands to empale my brow.
The learn'd in love say, Thus the winged boy
Does first approach, dressed up in welcome joy;
At first he to the cheated lover's sight
Naught represents, but rapture and delight,

Alluring hopes, soft fears, which stronger bind
Their hearts, than when they more assurance find. 30

Emboldened thus, to Fame I did commit
(By some few hands) my most unlucky wit.
But, ah, the sad effects that from it came!
What ought t'have brought me honour, brought me shame!
Like Aesop's painted jay I seemed to all,
Adorned in plumes I not my own could call:
Rifled like her, each one my feathers tore,
And, as they thought, unto the owner bore.
My laurels thus an other's brow adorned,
My numbers they admired, but me they scorned: 40
An other's brow, that had so rich a store
Of sacred wreaths, that circled it before;
Where mine quite lost, (like a small stream that ran
Into a vast and boundless ocean)
Was swallowed up, with what it joined and drowned,
And that abyss yet no accession found.

Orinda, (Albion's and her sex's grace)
Owed not her glory to a beauteous face,
It was her radiant soul that shone within.
Which struck a lustre through her outward skin; 50
That did her lips and cheeks with roses dye,
Advanced her height, and sparkled in her eye.
Nor did her sex at all obstruct her fame,
But higher 'mong the stars it fixed her name;
What she did write, not only all allowed,
But ev'ry laurel to her laurel bowed!

Th'envious age, only to me alone
Will not allow, what I write, my own,
But let 'em rage, and 'gainst a maid conspire,
So deathless numbers from my tuneful lyre 60
Do ever flow; so Phoebus I by thee
Divinely inspired and possessed may be;
I willingly accept Cassandra's fate,
To speak the truth, although believed too late.

ANNE FINCH
COUNTESS OF WINCHILSEA
1661-1720

Her father, Sir William Kingsmill, died before her birth, her mother Anne (Hazlewood) and stepfather, Sir Thomas Ogle, during her childhood; she survived, to become Maid of Honour to Mary of Modena, and marry, in 1684 (registering herself as 'spinster aged about 18 years') Col. Heneage Finch, a Court officer: the marriage was childless but very happy. When James II was deposed they retired to the Kent country seat of the Earl of Winchilsea, to which title Finch expectedly succeeded in 1712. Lived a retired, country life; published her poems anonymously, praising the virtues of having 'the skill to write, the modesty to hide'. In some respects a typical Augustan poet of society – she knew Pope and Gay (who mocked her in *Three Hours after Marriage* as Phoebe Clinket, ink-stained and with pens in her hair): conjugal life, women's friendship, nature and retirement constituted major themes. Wordsworth made an anthology of her poetry.

Miscellany Poems On Several Occasions (London, 1713); Myra Reynolds (ed.), *The Poems of Anne, Countess of Winchilsea* (Chicago: Chicago UP, 1903); Katharine N. Rogers, *Six Eighteenth-Century Women Authors* (NY: Frederick Ungar, 1979).

*The Introduction**

Did I intend my lines for public view,
How many censures would their faults pursue!
Some would, because such words they do affect,
Cry they're insipid, empty, incorrect.
And many have attained, dull and untaught,
The name of wit, only by finding fault.
True judges might condemn their want of wit;
And all might say, they're by a woman writ.
Alas! a woman that attempts the pen,
Such an intruder on the rights of men,   10
Such a presumptuous creature is esteemed,
The fault can by no virtue be redeemed.

They tell us we mistake our sex and way;
Good breeding, fashion, dancing, dressing, play,
Are the accomplishments we should desire;
To write, or read, or think, or to enquire,
Would cloud our beauty, and exhaust our time,
And interrupt the conquests of our prime;
Whilst the dull manage of a servile house
Is held by some our utmost art and use.   20
    Sure, 'twas not ever thus, nor are we told
Fables, of women that excelled of old;
To whom, by the diffusive hand of heaven,
Some share of wit and poetry was given.
On that glad day, on which the Ark returned,
The holy pledge, for which the land had mourned,
The joyful tribes attend it on the way,
The Levites do the sacred charge convey,
Whilst various instruments before it play;
Here, holy virgins in the concert join,   30
The louder notes to soften and refine,
And with alternate verse complete the hymn divine.
    Lo! the young poet, after God's own heart,
By Him inspired and taught the Muses' art,
Returned from conquest a bright chorus meets,
That sing his slain ten thousand in the streets.
In such loud numbers they his acts declare,
Proclaim the wonders of his early war,
That Saul upon the vast applause does frown,
And feels its mighty thunder shake the crown.   40
What can the threatened judgement now prolong?
Half of the kingdom is already gone:
The fairest half, whose judgement guides the rest,
Have David's empire o'er their hearts confessed.
    A woman here leads fainting Israel on,
She fights, she wins, she triumphs with a song,
Devout, majestic, for the subject fit,
And far above her arms, exalts her wit,
Then to the peaceful, shady palm withdraws,

And rules the rescued nation with her laws.   50
   How are we fallen! fall'n by mistaken rules,
And education's, more than Nature' fools;
Debarred from all improvements of the mind,
And to be dull, expected and designed;
And if some one would soar above the rest,
With warmer fancy, and ambition pressed,
So strong th'opposing faction still appears,
The hopes to thrive can ne'er outweigh the fears.
Be cautioned, then, my Muse, and still retired;
Nor be despised, aiming to be admired;   60
Conscious of wants, still with contracted wing,
To some few friends, and to thy sorrows sing.
For groves of laurel thou wert never meant:
Be dark enough thy shades, and be thou there content.

A Letter to Daphnis

This to the crown and blessing of my life,
The much loved husband of a happy wife;
To him whose constant passion found the art
To win a stubborn and ungrateful heart,
And to the world by tenderest proof discovers
They err, who say that husbands can't be lovers.
With such return of passion as is due,
Daphnis I love, Daphnis my thoughts pursue;
Daphnis, my hopes and joys are bounded all in you.
Even, I for Daphnis' and my promise' sake,   10
What I in women censure, undertake.
But this from love, not vanity, proceeds;
You know who writes, and I who 'tis that reads.
Judge not my passion by my want of skill:
Many love well, though they express it ill;
And I your censure could with pleasure bear,
Would you but soon return, and speak it here.

from *The Spleen. A Pindaric Poem**

What art thou, Spleen, which everything dost ape?
   Thou Proteus to abused mankind,
   Who never yet thy real cause could find
Or fix thee to remain in one continued shape.
   Still varying thy perplexing form
   Now a Dead Sea thou'lt represent,
   A calm of stupid discontent,
Then, dashing on the rocks, with rage into a storm.
   Trembling sometimes thou dost appear
   Dissolved into a panic fear;   10
   Or sleep intruding dost thy shadows spread
And crowd with boding dreams the melancholy head;
   Or when the midnight hour is told
   And drooping lids thou still dost waking hold,
   Thy fond delusions cheat the eyes;
   Before them antic spectres dance,
Unusual fires their pointed heads advance
   And airy phantoms rise.
   Such was the monstrous vision seen
When Brutus (now beneath his cares oppressed   20
And all Rome's fortunes rolling in his breast
   Before Philippi's latest field,
Before his fate did to Octavius yield)
   Was vanquished by the Spleen.

   Falsely, the mortal part we blame
   Of our depressed and ponderous frame,
   Which, till the first degrading sin
   Let thee its dull attendant in,
   Still with the other did comply
Nor clogged the active soul, disposed to fly   30
And range the mansions of its native sky.
   Nor whilst in his own heaven he dwelt
   Whilst Man his Paradise possessed,
His fertile garden in the fragrant east,

And all united odours smelt,
No armed sweets until thy reign
Could shock the sense, or in the face
A flushed, unhandsome colour place.
Now the jonquil o'ercomes the feeble brain;
We faint beneath the aromatic pain,   40
Till some offensive scent thy powers appease,
And pleasure we resign for short and nauseous ease.

In every one thou dost possess
New are thy motions and thy dress;
Now in some grove a listening friend
Thy false suggestions must attend,
Thy whispered griefs, thy fancied sorrows hear,
Breathed in a sigh and witnessed by a tear;
Whilst in the light and vulgar crowd
Thy slaves, more clamorous and loud,   50
By laughters unprovoked thy influence too confess.
In the imperious wife thou Vapours art,
Which from o'erheated passions rise
In clouds to the attractive brain
Until, descending thence again,
Through the o'ercast and showering eyes,
Upon her husband's softened heart,
He the disputed point must yield,
Something resign of the contested field;
Till lordly man, born to imperial sway,   60
Compounds for peace, to make that right away
And woman, armed with spleen, does servilely obey.

The fool, to imitate the wits,
Complains of thy pretended fits,
And dullness, born with him, would lay
Upon thy accidental sway;
Because sometimes thou dost presume
Into the ablest heads to come:
That often men of thoughts refined,

Impatient of unequal sense,   70
Such slow returns where they so much dispense,
Retiring from the crowd, are to thy shades inclined.
    O'er me, alas! thou dost too much prevail:
I feel thy force whilst I against thee rail:
Through thy black jaundice I all objects see
    As dark, as terrible as thee,
My lines decried, and my employment thought
An useless folly or presumptuous fault:
    Whilst in the Muses' path I stray,   80
Whilst in their groves and by their secret springs
My hand delights to trace unusual things,
And deviates from the known and common way;
    Nor will in fading silks compose
    Faintly the inimitable rose,
Fill up an ill-drawn bird, or paint on glass
The Sovereign's blurred and undistinguished face,
The threatening angel and the speaking ass.

Patron thou art to every gross abuse,
    The sullen husband's feigned excuse
When the ill-humour with his wife he spends   90
And bears recruited wit and spirits to his friends.
    The son of Bacchus pleads thy power
    As to the glass he still repairs,
    Pretends but to remove thy cares,
Snatch from thy shades one gay and smiling hour
And drown thy kingdom in a purple shower.
When the coquette, whom every fool admires,
    Would in variety be fair,
    And changing hastily the scene   100
    From light, impertinent and vain,
Assumes a soft, a melancholy air,
And of her eyes rebates the wandering fires,
The careless posture and the head reclined,
    The thoughtful and composed face,
Proclaiming the withdrawn, the absent mind,

Allows the fop more liberty to gaze,
Who gently for the tender cause inquires.
The cause, indeed is a defect in sense,
Yet is the spleen alleged and still the dull pretence [. . .]   110

The Unequal Fetters*

Could we stop the time that's flying
   Or recall it when 'tis past,
Put far off the day of dying
   Or make youth for ever last,
To love would then be worth our cost.

But since we must lose those graces
   Which at first your hearts have won
And you seek for in new faces
   When our spring of life is done,
It would but urge our ruin on.   10

Free as Nature's first intention
   Was to make us, I'll be found,
Nor by subtle Man's invention
   Yield to be in fetters bound
By one that walks a freer round.

Marriage does but slightly tie men
   Whilst close prisoners we remain,
They the larger slaves of Hymen
   Still are begging love again
At the full length of all their chain.   20

A Nocturnal Reverie*

In such a night, when every tender wind
Is to its distant cavern safe confined;
And only gentle Philomel, still waking, sings,
Or from some tree, famed for the owl's delight,
She, hollowing clear, directs the wand'rer right;
In such a night, when passing clouds give place,
Or thinly veil the heaven's mysterious face;
When in some river, overhung with green,
The waving moon and trembling leaves are seen;   10
When freshened grass now bears itself upright,
And makes cool banks to pleasing rest invite,
Whence springs the woodbind and the bramble-rose,
And where the sleepy cowslip sheltered grows;
Whilst now a paler hue the foxglove takes,
Yet chequers still with red the dusky brakes;
When scattered glow-worms, but in twilight fine,
Show trivial beauties, watch their hour to shine;
Whilst Salisb'ry stands the test of every light,
In perfect charms and perfect virtue bright;   20
When odours, which declined repelling day,
Through temp'rate air uninterrupted stray;
When darkened groves their softest shadows wear,
And falling waters we distinctly hear;
When through the gloom more venerable shows
Some ancient fabric, awful in repose,
While sunburnt hills their swarthy looks conceal,
And swelling haycocks thicken up the vale;
When the loosed horse now, as his pasture leads,
Comes slowly grazing through th'adjoining meads,   30
Whose stealing pace and lengthened shade we fear,
Till torn-up forage in his teeth we hear;
When nibbling sheep at large pursue their food,
And unmolested kine rechew the cud;
When curlews cry beneath the village walls,
And to her straggling brood the partridge calls;

Their short-lived jubilee the creatures keep,
Which but endures whilst tyrant man does sleep;
When a sedate content the spirit feels,
And no fierce light disturbs, whilst it reveals,   **40**
But silent musings urge the mind to seek
Something too high for syllables to speak;
Till the free soul to a compos'dness charmed,
Finding the elements of rage disarmed,
O'er all below a solemn quiet grown,
Joys in th'inferior world and thinks it like her own:
In such a night let me abroad remain,
Till morning breaks, and all's confused again:
Our cares, our toils, our clamours are renewed,
Or pleasures, seldom reached, again pursued.   **50**

SARAH FYGE EGERTON
1669-1723

> What cross impetuous Planets govern me,
> That I'm thus hurry'd on to Misery.

Her riposte to Robert Gould's misogynist satire, *Love Given O're* (1682)
was published in 1686 and again in 1687; she was sent away from home
by her father, Thomas Fyge, apothecary, and married off to an attorney,
Edward Field, who died *c*.1695; despite a fancy for Field's married clerk,
she then married a much older cousin, The Revd Thomas Egerton. The
marriage developed unhappily (a meat pie was thrown), and both parties
petitioned for divorce, unsuccessfully, in 1703. The woman playwright
Delariviere Manley pitied the 'old thin raw-bon'd Priest' married to 'a
she-Devil incarnate...in love with all the handsome Fellows...flat-
nos'd, blubber-lipp'd'.

*The Female Advocate, or, an Answere to a late Satyr against the Pride, Lust
and Inconstancy, etc., of Woman* (London, 1686); *Poems on Several Occasions,
together with a pastoral* (London, 1703); *A Collection of Poems* (London,
1706).

from *The Female Advocate*
*Or, An Answer to a Late Satyr**

Blasphemous wretch! How canst thou think or say
Some cursed or banished fiend usurped the sway
When Eve was formed? For then's denied by you
God's omnipresence and omniscience too:
Without which attributes he could not be
The greatest and supremest deity:
Nor can Heav'n sleep, though it may mourn to see
Degen'rate man speak such vile blasphemy.

When from dark chaos Heav'n the world did make,
And all was glorious it did undertake;   10
Then were in Eden's garden freely placed
Each thing that's pleasant to the sight or taste,
'Twas filled with beasts and birds, trees hung with fruit,

That might with man's celestial nature suit:
The world being made thus spacious and complete,
Then man was formed, who seemed nobly great.
When Heav'n surveyed the works that it had done,
Saw male and female, but found man alone,
A barren sex, and insignificant,
Then Heav'n made woman to supply the want,   20
And to make perfect what before was scant:
Surely then she a noble creature is,
Whom Heav'n thus made to consummate all bliss.
Though man had being first, yet methinks she
In nature should have the supremacy;
For man was formed out of dull senseless earth,
But woman had a much more noble birth:
For when the dust was purified by Heaven,
Made into man, and life unto it was given,
Then the almighty and all-wise God said,   30
That woman of that species should be made;
Which was no sooner said, but it was done,
'Cause 'twas not fit for man to be alone.

Thus have I proved woman's creation good,
And not inferior, when right understood,
To that of man's; for both one maker had,
Which made all good; then how could Eve be bad?
But then you'll say, though she at first was pure,
Yet in that state she did not long endure.
'Tis true; but yet her fall examine right;   40
We find most men have banished truth for spite:
Nor is she quite so guilty as some make,
For Adam most did of the guilt partake;
While he from God's own mouth had the command,
But woman had it at the second hand:
The Devil's strength weak woman might deceive
But Adam only tempted was by Eve:
She had the strongest tempter, and least charge;
Man's knowing most, doth make his sin more large.

109

But though that woman man to sin did lead,   50
Yet since her seed hath bruised the Serpent's head:
Why should she thus be made a public scorn,
Of whom the great almighty God was born?
Surely to speak one slighting word, must be
A kind of murmuring impiety:
But yet their greatest haters still prove such
Who formerly have loved them too much;
And from the proverb are they not exempt,
Too much familiarity has bred contempt.
They make all base for one's immodesty;   60
Nay, make the name a kind of magic spell,
As if 'twould conjure married men to Hell.

Woman! By Heaven, the very name's a charm,
And will my verse against all critics arm [. . .]

. . . I am not sorry you do females hate,
But rather deem ourselves more fortunate,
Because I find, when you're right understood,
You are at enmity with all that's good,
And should you love them, I should think they were
A-growing bad, but still keep as you are: 70
I need not bid you, for you must I'm sure,
And in your present wretched state endure;
'Tis as impossible you should be true,
As for a woman to act like to you,
Which I am sure will not accomplished be,
Till heaven's turned hell, and that's repugnancy;
When vice turns virtue, then 'tis you shall have
A share of that which makes most females brave;
Which transmutations I am sure can't be;
So thou must lie in vast eternity,   80
With prospect of thy endless misery,
When woman, your imagined fiend, shall live
Blessed with the joys that Heaven can always give.

The Liberty*

Shall I be one of those obsequious fools,
That square their lives by Custom's scanty rules;
Condemned for ever to the puny curse,
Of precepts taught, at boarding-school, or nurse,
That all the business of my life must be
Foolish, dull, trifling, formality.
Confined to a strict magic complaisance,
And round a circle of nice visits dance,
Nor for my life beyond the chalk advance:
The devil Censure stands to guard the same,   10
One step awry, he tears my vent'rous fame.
So when my friends, in a facetious vein,
With mirth and wit, a while can entertain;
Though ne'er so pleasant, yet I must not stay,
If a commanding clock bids me away:
But with a sudden start, as in a fright,
I must be gone indeed, 'tis after eight.
Sure these restraints, with such regret we bear,
That dreaded censure, can't be more severe,
Which has no terror, if we did not fear;   20
But let the bug-bear tim'rous infants fright,
I'll not be scared from innocent delight:
Whatever is not vicious, I dare do,
I'll never to the idol Custom bow,
Unless it suits with my own humour too.
Some boast their fetters of formality,
Fancy they ornamental bracelets be,
I'm sure they're gyves, and manacles to me.
To their dull fulsome rules, I'd not be tied,
For all the flattery that exalts their pride: 30
My sex forbids I should my silence break,
I lose my jest, 'cause women must not speak.
Mysteries must not be with my search prophaned,
My closet not with books, but sweet-meats crammed,
A little china, to advance the show,

111

My Prayer Book, and Seven Champions, or so.
My pen if ever used employed must be
In lofty themes of useful housewifery,
Transcribing old receipts of cookery:
And what is necessary 'mongst the rest,   40
Good cure for agues, and a cancered breast;
But I can't here write my *Probatum est*.
My daring pen will bolder sallies make,
And like my self, an unchecked freedom take;
Not chained to the nice order of my sex,
And with restraints my wishing soul perplex:
I'll blush at sin, and not what some call shame,
Secure my virtue, slight precarious fame.
This courage speaks me brave, 'tis surely worse
To keep those rules which privately we curse: 50
And I'll appeal to all the formal saints,
With what reluctance they endure restraints.

*The Emulation**

Say tyrant Custom, why must we obey
The impositions of thy haughty sway;
From the first dawn of life, unto the grave,
Poor womankind's in every state, a slave.
The nurse, the mistress, parent and the swain,
For love she must, there's none escape that pain;
Then comes the last, the fatal slavery,
The husband with insulting tyranny
Can have ill manners justified by law;
For men all join to keep the wife in awe.   10
Moses who first our freedom did rebuke,
Was married when he writ the Pentateuch;
They're wise to keep us slaves, for well they know,
If we were loose, we soon should make them, so.
We yield like vanquished kings whom fetters bind,
When chance of war is to usurpers kind:

Submit in form; but they'd our thoughts control,
And lay restraints on the impassive soul:
They fear we should excel their sluggish parts,
Should we attempt the sciences and arts.   20
Pretend they were designed for them alone,
So keep us fools to raise their own renown;
Thus priests of old their grandeur to maintain,
Cried vulgar eyes would sacred laws prophane.
So kept the mysteries behind a screen,
Their homage and the name were lost had they been seen:
But in this blessed age, such freedom's given,
That every man explains the will of heaven;
And shall we women now sit tamely by,
Make no excursions in philosophy,   30
Or grace our thoughts in tuneful poetry?
We will our rights in learning's world maintain,
Wit's empire, now, shall know a female reign;
Come all ye fair, the great attempt improve,
Divinely imitate the realms above:
There's ten celestial females govern wit,
And but two gods that do pretend to it;
And shall these finite males reverse their rules?
No, we'll be wits, and then men must be fools.

ELIZABETH SINGER ROWE
1674-1737

Born in Ilchester, Somerset, eldest daughter of Elizabeth (Portnell) and Walter Singer, a dissenting preacher (who met when he was imprisoned for Nonconformity). Well educated; began writing verse at twelve; was patronized by the family of Henry Thynne of Longleat; first in print in 1693. In 1710 married Thomas Rowe, thirteen years her junior, who died of consumption in 1715; her elegy on his death inspired Pope's *Eloisa to Abelard*. Later suppressed the erotic element in her verse, as she became more pious in her retirement in Frome; became a celebrated writer of uplifting prose, and of lifeless devotional verse. She seems not to have been a cheery old lady: when told that she looked well and should live long, she replied 'that it was the same as telling a slave his fetters were like to be lasting, or complimenting him on the walls of his dungeon'.

Poems on Several Occasions. Written by Philomela (London, 1696); T. Rowe (ed.), *The Miscellaneous Works in Prose and Verse of Mrs Elizabeth Singer* (London, 1739); Henry F. Stecher, *Elizabeth Singer Rowe: The Poetess of Frome. A Study in Eighteenth-Century English Pietism* (Frankfurt: M. Peter Lang; Bern: Herbert Land, 1973).

To Celinda

I

I can't, Celinda, say, I love,
 But rather I adore,
When with transported eyes I view
 Your *shining* merits o'er.

II

A frame so spotless and serene,
 A virtue so refined;
And thoughts as great, as e'er was yet
 Grasped by a *female mind*.

III

There love and honour dressed in all
    Their *genuine charms* appear,   **10**
And with a pleasing force at once
    They conquer and endear.

IV

Celestial flames are scarce more bright,
    Than those your worth inspires,
So Angels love and so they burn
    In just such holy fires.

V

Then let's my dear *Celinda* thus
    Blest in our selves contemn
The treacherous and deluding arts,
    Of those *base things called men*.   **20**

The Expostulation

I

How long, great God, a wretched captive here,
Must I these hated marks of bondage wear?
How long shall these uneasy chains control
The willing flights of my impatient soul?
How long shall her most pure intelligence
Be strained through an infectious screen of gross, corrupted
    sense?

II

When shall I leave this darksome house of clay;
And to a brighter mansion wing away?
There's nothing here my thoughts to entertain,
But one tired revolution o'er again: **10**
The sun and stars observe their wonted round,
The streams their former courses keep: no novelty is found.

III

The same curst acts of false fruition o'er,
The same wild hopes and wishes as before;
Do men for this so fondly life caress,
(That airy huff of splendid emptiness?)
Unthinking sots: kind Heaven let me be gone,
I'm tired, I'm sick of this dull farce's repetition.

from *To one that persuades me to leave the Muses**

Forgo the charming Muses! No, in spite
Of your ill-natured prophecy I'll write,
And for the future paint my thoughts at large,
I waste no paper at the Hundred's charge:
I rob no neighbouring geese of quills, nor slink
For a collection to the church for ink:
Besides my Muse is the most gentle thing
That ever yet made an attempt to sing:
I call no lady punk, nor gallants fops,
Nor set the married world on edge for ropes;   10
Yet I'm so scurvily inclined to rhyming,
That undesigned my thoughts burst out a-chiming;
My active Genius will by no means sleep,
And let it then its proper channel keep.
I've told you, and you may believe me too,
That I must this, or greater mischief do;
And let the world think me inspired, or mad,
I'll surely write while paper's to be had;
Since Heaven to me has a retreat assigned,
That would inspire a less harmonious mind.   20
All that a poet loves I have in view,
Delightsome hills, refreshing shades, and pleasant valleys too;
Fair spreading valleys clothed with lasting green,
And sunny banks with gilded streams between,
Gay as Elysium, in a lover's dream,
Or Flora's mansion, seated by a stream,

116

Where free from sullen cares I live at ease,
Indulge my Muse, and wishes, as I please,
Exempt from all that looks like want or strife,
I smoothly glide along the plains of life,   30
Thus Fate conspires, and what can I do to't?
Besides, I'm vehemently in love to boot,
And that there's not a willow sprig but knows,
In whose sad shade I breathe my direful woes,
But why for these dull reasons do I pause,
When I've at hand my genuine one, because!

    And that my Muse may take no counter spell,
I fairly bid the boarding schools farewell:
No young impertinent shall here intrude,
And vex me from this blissful solitude [. . .]   40
. . . Japan, and my esteemed pencil too,
And pretty Cupid, in the glass, adieu,
And since the dearest friends that be must part,
Old governess farewell with all my heart.
Now welcome all the inspiring tender things
That please my Genius, suit my make and years,
Unburdened yet with all but lover's cares.

To Orestes

To vex thy soul with these unjust alarms,
Fie dear mistrustful, canst thou doubt thy charms,
Or think a breast so young and soft as mine
Could e'er resist such charming eyes as thine?
Not love thee! witness all ye powers above,
(That know my heart) to what excess I love,
How many tender sighs for thee I've spent,
I who ne'er knew what serious passion meant,
Till to revenge his slighted votaries,
The God of Love, couched in thy beauteous eyes,   10
At once inspired and fixed my roving heart,
Which till that moment scorned his proudest dart.

117

And now I languish out my life for thee,
As others unregarded do for me;
Silent as night, and pensive as a dove,
Through shades more gloomy than my thoughts I rove,
With downcast eyes as languishing an air,
The emblem I of love, and of Despair.

from *A Paraphrase on the Canticles**

CHAPTER II
(1)
At thy approach, my cheek with blushes glows,
And conscious warmth, which with Thee comes and goes;
Like the pale lily joined to Sharon's rose;
And thorns to them I sooner would compare
Than other beauties to my darling fair.

(2)
And I as soon would rank a fruitful tree
With barren shrubs, as mortal clod with thee.
Beneath thy shade, blest, to my wish, I sate,
And of thy royal banquet freely eat;
Whilst o'er my head a banner was displayed: 10
In which, oh melting sight, the God of Love did bleed.
Excess of pleasure will my soul destroy;
I'm ev'n oppressed with the tyrannic joy:
Oh therefore turn thy lovely eyes away;
(Yet do not, for I die unless they stay.)
I faint, I faint; alas, no mortal yet
With eyes undazzled half this splendour met:
But sure I cannot sink, upheld by Thee;
So would I rest unto Eternity.
And now I charge you, Virgins, not to make   20
The least disturbance, till my Love awake.

(3)

What charming voice is that salutes my ear?
It must be my Beloved's: he is near:
He is, and yet unfriendly stays without:
He stays, as if he did a welcome doubt.
But hark, methinks I hear him softly say,
Arise my fair, arise, and come away!
For lo the stormy winter's past and gone;
And summer, dressed in all her pride, comes on:
The warbling birds in airy raptures sing   30
Their glad Pindarics to the welcome spring:
The fig-trees sprout, the cheerful vines look gay;
Arise my lovely fair, and come away!
Come forth, my dove, my charming innocence;
How canst thou fear, while I am thy defence?

(4)

Do thou the spiteful foxes then destroy,
That would my young aspiring vines annoy.
Not for the world would I exchange my bliss,
While my Beloved's mine, and I am His.
And till the break of that Eternal Day,   40
Whose rising Sun shall chase the shades away;
Turn my Beloved, turn again; and thy
Dear sight shall make the lazy moments fly.

from CHAPTER IV

(Bridegroom)
Though all the lower world should ransacked be,
There could be found no parallel for thee:
Thy eyes like doves, thy fair intangling locks,
Curled, and soft as Gilead's milky flocks:
Like them thy pearly teeth appear, for so
Unsullied from the crystal streams they go.
But oh! To what may I thy lips compare?

Since fragrant roses bloom not half so fair,
The morning ne'er with such a crimson blushed,
When from the arms of sooty night she rushed.   10
The ripe pomgranate's scarlets are but faint,
To those fresh beauties that thy cheeks do paint.
Thy neck and breasts, in whiteness, do out-go
Ungathered lilies, or descending snow.
And till the dawn of that expected Day,
When all my radiant glories I display,
And chase at once the injurious shades away:
I'll on the hills of frankincense reside,
And pass the time with thee my charming bride.

from CHAPTER V

(Daughters of Jerusalem)
What thy Beloved is, we first would know,
Fairest of women! thou dost charge us so.
What charms unequalled in him dost thou see,
Impatient fair! to raise these storms in thee?

(Spousa)
Commencing all perfection, he is such
Your most exalted thought can hardly touch,
Unsullied heaps of snow are not so white,
He's fairer than condensed beams of light,
His rosy cheeks of such a lucent dye,
As Sol ne'er gilded on the morning sky.   10
His head like unpolished gold, his graceful hair
Dark as the plumes that jetty ravens wear.
His eyes, the endless magazines of Love,
How soft! how sweet! how powerfully they move!
He breathes more sweetness than the infant morn,
When heavenly dews the flow'ry plains adorn.
The fragrant drops of rich Arabian gums
Burnt on the altar, yield not such perfumes.
His hands, surpassing lilies, graced with gems,

Fit to enrich celestial diadems.   20
His breast smooth ivory, enamelled all
With veins, which sapphires 'twere unjust to call.
Divine his steps, with his majestic air,
Not ev'n the lofty cedars can compare.
So sweet his voice, the list'ning angels throng
With silent harps to th'music of his tongue.
He's altogether—lovely, This is He,
Now, Virgins! Pity, though you envy me.

LADY MARY WORTLEY MONTAGU
1689-1762

Her father was Evelyn Pierrepoint, later Duke of Kingston; her mother, Lady Mary Fielding, died when she was young; educated by a governess, but taught herself Latin. In 1706 met Edward Wortley, a politician eleven years older; when her father tried to marry her off (to the Hon. Clotworthy Skeffington) the couple eloped on the wedding eve (1712). Lived in London, where they had Court connections; had two children, but the marriage faded away. Knew 'everybody'; Pope's *Eloise to Abelard* was directed at her, though he later turned against her (reputedly because she mocked his advances) and attacked her viciously – 'From furious Sappho scarce a milder fate, / P—x'd by her love, or libell'd by her hate'. In 1715 small-pox ruined her beauty, leaving her no eyelashes and a deeply pitted skin. Visited Constantinople (and the Sultan's seraglio) as Ambassador's wife; wrote verses and a political periodical. In 1736 became infatuated with a bisexual 24-year-old Italian, Francesco Algarotti, pursuing him (unsuccessfully) to Europe, travelling with thirteen cases, including furniture and some five hundred books. For the next twenty years lived abroad, returning only on her husband's death. Horace Walpole described her as 'not handsome, had a wild staring eye, was much marked with the smallpox, which she endeavoured to conceal by filling up the depressions with white paint'.

Robert Halsband and Isobel Grundy (eds.), *Lady Mary Wortley Montagu: Essays and Poems, and Simplicity, a Comedy* (Oxford: Clarendon, 1977); Robert Halsband, *The Life of Mary Wortley Montagu* (Oxford: Clarendon, 1956).

from *Six Town Eclogues**

SATURDAY: THE SMALL POX

Flavia

The wretched Flavia, on her couch reclined,
Thus breathed the anguish of a wounded mind.
A glass reversed in her right hand she bore;
For now she shunned the face she sought before.
  How am I changed! Alas, how am I grown

A frightful spectre to my self unknown!
Where's my complexion, where the radiant bloom
That promised happiness for years to come?
Then, with what pleasure I this face surveyed!
To look once more, my visits oft delayed!   10
Charmed with the view, a fresher red would rise,
And a new life shot sparkling from my eyes.
Ah faithless glass, my wonted bloom restore!
Alas, I rave! that bloom is now no more!

   The greatest good the gods on men bestow,
Even youth it self to me is useless now.
There was a time, (Oh that I could forget!)
When opera tickets poured before my feet,
And at the Ring where brightest beauties shine,
The earliest cherries of the park were mine.   20
Witness oh Lilly! and thou Motteux tell!
How much Japan these eyes have made you sell,
With what contempt you saw me oft despise
The humble offer of the raffled prize:
For at each raffle still the prize I bore,
With scorn rejected, or with triumph wore;
Now beauty's fled, and presents are no more.

   For me, the patriot has the House forsook,
And left debates to catch a passing look,
For me, the soldier has soft verses writ,   30
For me, the beau has aimed to be a wit,
For me, the wit to nonsense was betrayed,
The gamester has for me his dun delayed,
And overseen the card, I would have paid.
The bold and haughty, by success made vain,
Awed by my eyes has trembled to complain,
The bashful squire touched with a wish unknown
Has dared to speak with spirit not his own,
Fired with one wish, all did alike adore,
Now beauty's fled, and lovers are no more.   40

   As round the room I turn my weeping eyes,
New unaffected scenes of sorrow rise;

123

Far from my sight that killing picture bear,
The face disfigure, or the canvas tear!
That picture, which with pride I used to show,
The lost resemblance but upbraids me now.
And thou my toilette! where I oft have sate,
While hours unheeded passed in deep debate,
How curls should fall, or where a patch to place,
If blue or scarlet best became my face;   50
Now on some happier nymph thy aid bestow,
On fairer heads, ye useless jewels, glow!
No borrowed lustre can my charms restore,
Beauty is fled, and dress is now no more.

    Ye meaner beauties, I permit you, shine,
Go triumph in the hearts, that once were mine,
But midst your triumphs, with confusion know,
'Tis to my ruin all your charms ye owe.
Would pitying Heaven restore my wonted mien,
You still might move, unthought of, and unseen –   60
But oh, how vain, how wretched is the boast,
Of beauty faded, and of empire lost!
What now is left, but weeping to deplore
My beauty fled, and empire now no more!

    Ye cruel chemists, what withheld your aid?
Could no pomatums save a trembling maid?
How false and trifling is that art you boast;
No art can give me back my beauty lost!
In tears surrounded by my friends I lay,
Masked o'er, and trembling at the light of day;   70
Mirmillo came my fortune to deplore
(A golden headed cane, well carved he bore),
Cordials, he cried, my spirits must restore, –
Beauty is fled, and spirit is no more!
Galen the grave, officious Squirt was there,
With fruitless grief and unavailing care;
Machaon too, the great Machaon, known
By his red cloak, and his superior frown,
And why (he cried) this grief, and this despair?

You shall again be well, again be fair,   80
Believe my oath (with that an oath he swore),
False was his oath! my beauty is no more.
    Cease hapless maid, no more thy tale pursue,
Forsake mankind, and bid the world adieu.
Monarchs, and beauties rule with equal sway,
All strive to serve, and glory to obey,
Alike unpitied when deposed they grow,
Men mock the idol of their former vow.
    Adieu ye Parks, in some obscure recess,
Where gentle streams will weep at my distress,   90
Where no false friend will in my grief take part,
And mourn my ruin with a joyful heart,
There let me live, in some deserted place,
There hide in shades this lost inglorious face.
Ye operas, circles, I no more must view!
My toilette, patches, all the world, adieu!

The Lover, A Ballad*

1

At length by so much importunity pressed,
Take (Molly) at once the inside of my breast,
This stupid indifference so often you blame
Is not owing to nature, to fear, or to shame,
I am not as cold as a virgin in lead,
Nor is Sunday's sermon so strong in my head,
I know but too well how time flies along,
That we live but few years and yet fewer are young.

2

But I hate to be cheated, and never will buy
Long years of repentance for moments of joy.   10
Oh was there a man (but where shall I find
Good sense, and good nature so equally joined?)
Would value his pleasure, contribute to mine,

125

Not meanly would boast, nor lewdly design,
Not over severe, yet not stupidly vain,
For I would have the power though not give the pain.

3
No pedant yet learned, not rakehelly gay
Or laughing because he has nothing to say,
To all my whole sex, obliging and free,
Yet never be fond of any but me.   20
In public preserve the decorums are just
And show in his eyes he is true to his trust,
Then rarely approach, and respectfully bow,
Yet not fulsomely pert, nor yet foppishly low.

4
But when the long hours of public are past
And we meet with champagne and a chicken at last,
May every fond pleasure that hour endear,
Be banished afar both discretion and fear,
Forgetting or scorning the airs of the crowd
He may cease to be formal, and I to be proud,   30
Till lost in the joy we confess that we live,
And he may be rude, and yet I may forgive.

5
And that my delight may be solidly fixed
Let the friend, and the lover be handsomely mixed,
In whose tender bosom my soul might confide,
Whose kindness can soothe me, whose counsel could guide,
From such a dear lover as here I describe
No danger should fright me, no millions should bribe,
But till this astonishing creature I know,
As I long have lived chaste I will keep myself so.   40

6
I never will share with the wanton coquette,
Or be caught by a vain affectation of wit.

The toasters, and songsters may try all their art
But never shall enter the pass of my heart;
I loathe the lewd rake, the dressed fopling despise,
Before such pursuers the wise virgin flies,
And as Ovid has sweetly in parables told,
We harden like trees, and like rivers are cold.

A Receipt to Cure the Vapours

Why will Delia thus retire
    And languish life away?
While the sighing crowds admire,
    'Tis too soon for hartshorn tea.

All these dismal looks and fretting
    Cannot Damon's life restore,
Long ago the worms have ate him,
    You can never see him more.

Once again consult your toilette,
    In the glass your face review,   10
So much weeping soon will spoil it
    And no spring your charms renew.

I like you was born a woman —
    Well I know what vapours mean,
The disease alas! is common,
    Single we have all the spleen.

All the morals that they tell us
    Never cured sorrow yet,
Choose among the pretty fellows
    One of humour, youth and wit.   20

Prithee hear him ev'ry morning
At least an hour or two,
Once again at nights returning,
I believe the dose will do.

'Between your sheets'*

Between your sheets you soundly sleep
Nor dream of vigils that we lovers keep
While all the night, I waking sigh your name,
The tender sound does every nerve inflame,
Imagination shows me all your charms,
The plenteous silken hair, and waxen arms,
The well turned neck, and snowy rising breast
And all the beauties that supinely rest
                        between your sheets.

Ah Lindamira, could you see my heart,   10
How fond, how true, how free from fraudful art,
The warmest glances poorly do explain
The eager wish, the melting throbbing pain
Which through my very blood and soul I feel,
Which you cannot believe nor I reveal,
Which every metaphor must render less
And yet (methinks) which I could well express
                        between your sheets.

MARY COLLIER
1689/90-after 1762

Born near Midhurst, Sussex, of 'poor, but honest Parents'; worked as an agricultural labourer, laundress and domestic servant until, aged sixty-three, she became a farm housekeeper; in 1762 was reported living in a garret in Alton. *The Womans Labour*, a poem suggesting some sophistication, provides a very emphatic reminder of the realities of pre-industrial labouring life.

Poems on Several Occasions (London, 1736; Winchester, 1762); *The Womans Labour: an epistle to Mr. Stephen Duck, in answer to his late poem, called 'The Thresher's Labour'* (London, 1739); *The Poems of Mary Collier* (Petersfield, 1765). Felicity Nussbaum and Laura Brown (eds), *The New Eighteenth Century* (London and NY: Methuen, 1987).

*The Womans Labour, an epistle**

Immortal Bard! thou fav'rite of the Nine!
Enriched by peers, advanced by Caroline!
Deign to look down on one that's poor and low,
Rememb'ring you yourself was lately so;
Accept these lines; Alas! what can you have
From her, who ever was, and's still a slave?
No learning ever was bestowed on me;
My life was always spent in drudgery:
And not alone; alas! with grief I find,
It is the portion of poor woman-kind.   10
Oft have I thought as on my bed I lay,
Eased from the tiresome labours of the day,
Our first extraction from a mass refined,
Could never be for slavery designed;
Till time and custom by degrees destroyed
That happy state our sex at first enjoyed.
When men had used their utmost care and toil,
Their recompence was but a female smile;
When they by arts or arms were rendered great,
They laid their trophies at a woman's feet;   20

They, in those days, unto our sex did bring
Their hearts, their all, a free-will offering;
And as from us their being they derive,
They back again should all due homage give.

Jove once descending from the clouds did drop
In showers of gold on lovely Danae's lap;
The sweet-tongued poets, in those generous days,
Unto our shrine still offered up their lays:
But now, alas! that Golden Age is past,
We are the objects of your scorn at last.   30
And you, great Duck, upon whose happy brow
The Muses seem to fix their garland now,
In your late poem boldly did declare
Alcides' labours can't with yours compare,
And of your annual task have much to say,
Of threshing, reaping, mowing corn and hay;
Boasting your daily toil, and nightly dream,
But can't conclude your never-dying theme
And let our hapless sex in silence lie
Forgotten, and in dark oblivion die,   40
But on our abject state you throw your scorn,
And women wrong, your verses to adorn.
You of hay-making speak a word or two,
As if our sex but little work could do:
This makes the honest farmer smiling say,
He'll seek for women still to make his hay,
For if his back be turned the work they mind
As well as men, as far as he can find.

For my own part, I many a summer's day
Have spent in throwing, turning, making hay;   50
But ne'er could see, what you have lately found,
Our wages paid for sitting on the ground.
'Tis true, that when our morning's work is done,
And all our grass exposed unto the sun,
While that his scorching beams do on it shine,

As well as you we have time to dine:
I hope, that since we freely toil and sweat
To earn our bread, you'll give us time to eat;
That over, soon we must get up again,
And nimbly turn our hay upon the plain;   60
Nay, rake and row it in, the case is clear,
Or how should cocks in equal rows appear?
But if you'd have what you have wrote believed,
I find, that you to hear us talk are grieved:
In this, I hope you do not speak your mind,
For none but Turks, that ever I could find,
Have mutes to serve them, or did e'er deny
Their slaves at work, to chat it merrily.
Since you have liberty to speak your mind,
And are to talk, as well as we, inclined,   70
Why should you thus repine, because that we,
Like you, enjoy that pleasing liberty?
What! would you lord it quite, and take away
The only privilege our sex enjoy?

When ev'ning does approach, we homeward hie
And our domestic toils incessant ply:
Against your coming home prepare to get
Our work all done, our house in order set;
Bacon and dumpling in the pot we boil,
Our beds we make, our swine we feed the while;   80
Then wait at door to see you coming home,
And set the table out against you come.
Early next morning we on you attend,
Our children dress and feed, their clothes we mend;
And in the field our daily task renew,
Soon as the rising sun has dried the dew.

When harvest comes, into the field we go,
And help to reap the wheat as well as you;
Or else we go the ears of corn to glean,
No labour scorning, be it e'er so mean;   90

131

But in the work we freely bear a part,
And what we can, perform with all our heart.
To get a living we so willing are,
Our tender babes unto the field we bear,
And wrap them in our clothes to keep them warm,
While round about we gather in the corn;
And often unto them our course do bend,
To keep them safe, that nothing them offend;
Our children that are able bear a share
In gleaning corn, such is our frugal care.   100
When night comes on, unto our home we go,
Our corn we carry, and our infant too,
Weary indeed! but 'tis not worth our while
Once to complain, or rest at ev'ry stile;
We must make haste, for when we home are come,
We find again our work but just begun;
So many things for our attendance call,
Had we ten hands, we could employ them all.
Our children put to bed, with greatest care
We all things for your coming home prepare: 110
You sup, and go to bed without delay,
And rest yourselves till the ensuing day;
While we, alas! but little sleep can have,
Because our froward children cry and rave;
Yet, without fail, soon as day-light doth spring,
We in the field again our work begin,
And there, with all our strength, our toil renew,
Till Titan's golden rays have dried the dew;
Then home we go unto our children dear,
Dress, feed, and bring them to the field with care.   120
Were this your case, you justly might complain
That day or night you are secure from pain;
Those mighty troubles which perplex your mind
(Thistles before, and females come behind)
Would vanish soon, and quickly disappear,
Were you, like us, encumbered thus with care.
What you would have of us we do not know:

We oft take up the corn that you do mow,
We cut the peas, and always ready are
In every work to take our proper share;   130
And from the time that harvest doth begin,
Until the corn be cut and carried in,
Our toil and labour's daily so extreme,
That we have hardly ever time to dream.

    The harvest ended, respite none we find;
The hardest of our toil is still behind;
Hard labour we most cheerfully pursue,
And out, abroad, a-charing often go,
Of which I now will briefly tell in part,
What fully to describe is past my art;   140
So many hardships daily we go through,
I boldly say, the like you never knew.

    When bright Orion glitters in the skies
In winter nights, then early we must rise;
The weather ne'er so bad, wind, rain, or snow,
Our work appointed, we must rise and go,
While you on easy beds may lie and sleep,
Till light does through your chamber windows peep.
When to the house we come where we should go,
How to get in, alas! we do not know: 150
The maid quite tired with work the day before,
O'ercome with sleep; we standing at the door
Oppressed with cold, and often call in vain,
E'er to our work we can admittance gain;
But when from wind and weather we get in,
Briskly with courage we our work begin.
Heaps of fine linen we before us view,
Whereon to lay our strength and patience too;
Cambrics and muslins which our ladies wear,
Laces and edgings, costly, fine, and rare,   160
Which must be washed with utmost skill and care,
With holland shirts, ruffles and fringes too,

Fashions which our fore-fathers never knew.
For several hours here we work and slave,
Before we can one glimpse of day-light have;
We labour hard before the morning's past,
Because we fear the time runs on too fast.

At length bright Sol illuminates the skies,
And summons drowsy mortals to arise;
Then comes our mistress without fail,   170
And in her hand, perhaps, a mug of ale
To cheer our hearts, and also to inform
Herself what work is done that very morn;
Lays her commands upon us, that we mind
Her linen well, nor leave the dirt behind;
Nor this alone, but also to take care
We don't her cambrics nor her ruffles tear;
And these most strictly does of us require,
To save her soap, and sparing be of fire,
Tells us her charge is great, nay furthermore,   180
Her clothes are fewer than the time before.
Now we drive on, resolved our strength to try,
And what we can we do most willingly;
Until with heat and work, 'tis often known,
Not only sweat, but blood runs trickling down
Our wrists and fingers; still our work demands
The constant action of our lab'ring hands.

Now night comes on, from whence you have relief,
But that, alas! does but increase our grief:
With heavy hearts we often view the sun,
Fearing he'll set before our work be done,
For either in the morning, or at night,
We piece the summer's day with candle-light.
Though we all day with care our work attend,
Such is our fate, we know not when 'twill end;
When evening's come, you homeward take your way,
We, till our work is done, are forced to stay;

134

And after all our toil and labour past,
Six-pence or eight-pence pays us off at last;
For all our pains, no prospect can we see
Attend us, but old age and poverty.

    The washing is not all we have to do:
We often change for work as well as you.
Our mistress of her pewter doth complain,
And 'tis our part to make it clean again.
This work, though very hard and tiresome too,
Is not the worst we hapless females do:
When night comes on, and we quite weary are,
We scarce can count what falls unto our share;
Pots, kettles, sauce-pans, skillets, we may see,
Skimmers, and ladles, and such trumpery,
Brought in to make complete our slavery.
Though early in the morning 'tis begun,
'Tis often very late before we've done;
Alas! our labours never know no end,
On brass and iron we our strength must spend;
Our tender hands and fingers scratch and tear;
All this, and more, with patience we must bear.
Coloured with dirt and filth we now appear;
Your threshing sooty peas will not come near.
All the perfections woman once could boast,
Are quite obscured, and altogether lost.

    Once more our mistress sends to let us know
She wants our help, because the beer runs low;
Then in much haste for brewing we prepare,
The vessels clean, and scald with greatest care;
Often at midnight from our bed we rise,
At other times, ev'n that will not suffice;
Our work at ev'ning oft we do begin,
And ere we've done, the night comes on again.
Water we pump, the copper we must fill,
Or tend the fire; for if we e'er stand still,

Like you, when threshing, we a watch must keep,
Our wort boils over, if we dare to sleep.

But to rehearse all labour is in vain,
Of which we very justly might complain:
For us, you see, but little rest is found;
Our toil increases as the year runs round.
While you to Sisyphus yourselves compare,
With Danaus' daughters we may claim a share: 240
For while he labours hard against the hill,
Bottomless tubs of water they must fill.

So the industrious bees do hourly strive
To bring their loads of honey to the hive;
Their sordid owners always reap the gains,
And poorly recompense their toil and pains.

LAETITIA PILKINGTON
1712?-1750

Born in Dublin, the second child of Dr Van Lewen, a Dutch 'man mid-wife'. From the age of thirteen was pursued by Matthew Pilkington, a clergyman and writer, whom she married at seventeen. She was be-friended and encouraged by Swift; her husband abandoned her; she pursued him to London, but he divorced her in 1738, on what she claimed were false charges of adultery (the man in her bedroom in the middle of the night was, she claimed, waiting for her to finish reading a book he had lent her). Resilient, gamesome, never quite respectable (probably mistress to the painter Worsdale), she supported herself and her children in London as best she could, including writing verses in hopes of patron-age. The *Memoirs* (the last volume published posthumously) are gossipy, amused, not always credible, but consistently entertaining. Though bef-riended by Cibber and Richardson, she never escaped a scandalous repu-tation (when Swift broke off their friendship he called her 'the most profligate whore in either kingdom'), and died destitute.

Memoirs of Mrs. Letitia Pilkington, Wife to the Rev. Mr. Matthew Pilkington, Written by Herself, Wherein are occasionally interspersed, All her Poems, 3 vols (London and Dublin, 1749); *Mrs. Pilkington's Jests: or, The Cabinet of Wit and Humour* (London, 1759); Virginia Woolf, *The Common Reader* (London: Hogarth Press, 1925).

The Wish, By a Young Lady

I ask not wit, nor beauty do I crave,
Nor wealth, nor pompous titles wish to have;
But since, 'tis doomed through all degrees of life,
Whether a daughter, sister, or a wife;
That females should the stronger males obey,
And yield implicit to their lordly sway;
Since this, I say, is ev'ry woman's fate,
Give me a mind to suit my slavish state.

Dol and Roger

Nay, Doll, quoth Roger, now you're caught,
    I'll never let you go
Till you consent, – To what? says Doll,
    Zounds, Doll, why, do'stn't know?
She faintly screamed, and vowed she would
    If hurt, cry out aloud;
Ne'er fear, says he, then seized the fair,
    She sighed – and sighed – and vowed, –
A'nt I a Man, quoth Roger, ha!
    Me you need never doubt,   10
Now did I hurt you, Doll? quoth he,
    Or, pray? says Doll, did I cry out?

A Song

Strephon, your breach of faith and trust
    Affords me no surprise;
A man who grateful was, or just,
    Might make my wonder rise.

That heart to you so fondly tied,
    With pleasure wore its chain,
But from your cold neglectful pride,
    Found liberty again.

For this no wrath inflames my mind,
    My thanks are due to thee;   10
Such thanks as gen'rous victors find,
    Who set their captives free.

A Song

Lying is an occupation,
    Used by all who mean to rise;

Politicians owe their station,
    But to well concerted lies.

These to lovers give assistance,
    To ensnare the fair-one's heart;
And the virgin's best resistance
    Yields to this commanding art.

Study this superior science,
    Would you rise in Church or State;   10
Bid to Truth a bold defiance,
    'Tis the practice of the great.

Fair and Softly goes far
or, The Wary Physician*

A doctor, of great skill and fame,
Paulo Purganti was his name,
Had a good, comely, virtuous wife;
No woman led a better life:
She to intrigue was ev'n hard hearted:
She chuckled when a bawd was carted;
And thought the nation ne'er would thrive,
Till all the whores were burnt alive.
    On married men, that dared be bad,
She thought no mercy should be had;   10
They should be hanged, or starved, or flayed,
Or served like Romish priests in Swede.
In short, all lewdness she defied;
And stiff was her parochial pride.
    Yet, in an honest way, the dame
Was a great lover of that same;
And could from Scripture take her cue,
That husbands should give wives their due.
    Her prudence did so justly steer
Between the gay and the severe,   20

139

That, if in some regards, she chose
To curb poor Paulo in too close;
In others, she relaxed again,
And governed with a looser rein.
    Thus, though she strictly did confine
The doctor from excess of wine;
With oysters, eggs, and vermicelli,
She let him almost burst his belly:
Thus, drying coffee was denied;
But chocolate that want supplied;   30
And for tobacco – who could bear it?
Filthy concomitant of claret! –
(Blest resolution!) one might see
Eringo roots, and Bohea tea.
She often stroked the doctor's band,
And stroked his beard, and kissed his hand,
Kindly complained, that after noon
He went to pore on books too soon:
She held it wholesomer by much,
To rest a little on the couch;   40
About his waist in bed a-nights
She clung on close – for fear of sprites.
    The doctor understood the call,
But had not always wherewithal.
    The Lion's skin too short, you know,
(As Plutarch's *Morals* finely show)
Was lengthened by the Fox's tail;
And Art supplies, where Strength may fail.
    Unwilling then in arms to meet
The enemy he could not beat,   50
He strove to lengthen the campaign,
And save his forces by chicane.
Fabius, the Roman chief, who thus
By fair retreat grew Maximus,
Shows us, that all warrior can do,
With force superior is *cunctando*.
    One day, then, as the foe drew near,

With Love, and Joy, and Life, and Dear,
Our Don, who knew this tittle-tattle
Did, sure as trumpet, call to battle,   60
Thought it extremely *à propos*,
To ward against the coming blow:
To ward: But how? ay, there's the question:
Fierce the assault, unarmed the bastion.
    The doctor feigned a strange surprise;
He felt her pulse; he viewed her eyes;
That was too fast; these rolled too quick:
She was, he said, or would be sick:
He judged it absolutely good,
That she should purge, and cleanse her blood.   70
Spa-waters to that end were got:
If they passed easily or not,
What matters it? the lady's fever
Continued as violent as ever.
    For a distemper of this kind
(Blackmore and Hans are of my mind)
If once it youthful blood infects,
And chiefly of the female sex,
Is scarce removed by pill or potion;
Whate'er may be our doctor's notion.   80
    One luckless night then, as in bed
The doctor and the dame were laid,
Again this cruel fever came:
High pulse, short breath, and blood in flame.
What measures shall poor Paulo keep
    With Madam in this piteous taking?
She, like Macbeth, has murdered sleep,
    And won't allow him rest, though waking.
Sad state of matters! when we dare
Nor ask for peace, nor offer war: 90
Nor Livy nor Comines have shown,
What in this juncture may be done.
Grotius might own, that Paulo's case is
Harder, than any which he places

Amongst his *Belli*, and his *Pacis*.
He strove, alas, but strove in vain,
By dint of logic to maintain
That all the sex was born to grieve,
Down to her Ladyship from Eve.
He ranged his tropes, and preached up patience;   100
Backed his opinion with quotations,
Divines and moralists; and run on
Quite through from Seneca to Bunyan.
As much in vain he bid her try
To fold her arms, to close her eye;
Telling her, rest would do her good,
If any thing in Nature could:
So held the Greeks quite down from Galen,
Masters and princes of the calling:
So all our modern friends maintain,   110
(Though no great Greeks) in Warwick-lane.
    Reduce, my Muse, the wand'ring song:
A tale should never be too long.
    The more he talked, the more she burned,
And sighed, and tossed, and groaned, and turned:
At last, I wish, said she, my dear –
(And whispered something in his ear).
You wish! wish on, the doctor cries:
Lord! when will womankind be wise?
What! in your waters; are you mad?   120
Why, poison is not half so bad.
I'll do – but I give you warning;
You'll die before tomorrow morning. –
'Tis kind, my dear, what you advise,
The lady with a sigh replies:
But life, you know, at best is pain:
And death is what we should disdain.
So do it therefore, and adieu:
For I will die for love of you. –
Let wanton wives by death be scared: 130
But, to my comfort, I'm prepared.

MARY LEAPOR
1722-1746

> Though nature armed us for the growing ill
> With fraudful cunning and a headstrong will;
> Yet, with ten thousand follies to her charge,
> Unhappy woman's but a slave at large.

Born at Marston St Lawrence, Northamptonshire; her father, Philip Leapor, was gardener to Judge Sir John Blencowe. Began writing at about ten or eleven; admired Pope; helped by Bridget Fremantle ('Artemisia'), daughter of a local rector. Worked as cook-maid to a man who described her as 'extremely swarthy and quite emaciated, with a long crane-neck, and a short body, much resembling in shape a bass-viol', and a propensity to scribble while the meat burned. After her mother Anne's death, looked after her father, who profited from the publication of her poems after her death from measles. Blunden remarks on the 'ease and good-humour of her self-portraiture', and her eager concern with 'the human comedy, with men and women in their wisdom or their folly'.

Poems upon Several Occasions (London, 1748, 1751); Edmund Blunden, *A Northamptonshire Poetess: Mary Leapor* (Northampton, 1936).

from *Essay on Friendship*

To Artemisia. – 'Tis to her we sing,
For her once more we touch the founding string.
'Tis not to Cythera's reign nor Cupid's fires,
But sacred Friendship that our muse inspires.
A theme that suits Aemilia's pleasing tongue:
So to the fair ones I devote my song.

The wise will seldom credit all they hear,
Though saucy wits should tell thee with a sneer,
That women's friendships, like a certain fly,
Are hatched i'the morning and at ev'ning die.   10
'Tis true, our sex has been from early time
A constant topic for satiric rhyme:

Nor without reason – since we're often found
Or lost in passion, or in pleasures drowned:
And the fierce winds that bid the ocean roll,
Are less inconstant than a woman's soul:
Yet some there are that keep the mod'rate way,
Can think an hour, and be calm a day:
Who ne'er were known to start into a flame,
Turn pale or tremble at a losing game,   20
Run Chloe's shape or Delia's features down,
Or change complexion at Celinda's gown:
But still serene, compassionate and kind,
Walk through life's circuit with an equal mind.

Of all companions I would choose to shun
Such, whose blunt truths are like a bursting gun,
Who in a breath count all your follies o'er,
And close their lectures with a mirthful roar:
But reason here will prove the safest guide,
Extremes are dang'rous placed on either side.   30
A friend too soft will hardly prove sincere;
The wit's inconstant, and the learn'd severe.
Good breeding, wit, and learning, all conspire
To charm mankind and make the world admire,
Yet in a friend but serve an under part:
The main ingredient is an honest heart [. . .]

from *The Head-ache: To Aurelia*

Aurelia, when your zeal makes known
Each woman's failings but your own,
How charming Silvia's teeth decay,
And Celia's hair is turning grey:
Yet Celia gay has sparkling eyes,
But (to your comfort) is not wise:
Methinks you take a world of pains,
To tell us Celia has no brains.

Now you wise folk, who make such a pother
About the wit of one another,   10
With pleasure would your brains resign,
Did all your noddles ache like mine.
  Not cuckolds half my anguish know,
When budding horns begin to grow;
Nor battered skull of wrestling Dick,
Who late was drubbed at single-stick;
Not wretches that in fevers fry,
Not Sappho when her cap's awry,
E'er felt such tort'ring pangs as I;
Nor forehead of Sir Jeffrey Strife,   20
When smiling Cynthio kissed his wife [. . .]

  Just so, Aurelia, you complain
Of vapours, rheums, and gouty pain;
Yet I am patient, so should you,
For cramps and head-aches are our due:
We suffer justly for our crimes;
For scandal you, and I for rhymes [. . .]
  Yet there's a mighty diff'rence too,
Between the fate of me and you;
Though you with tott'ring age will bow,   30
And wrinkles scar your lovely brow;
Your busy tongue may still proclaim
The faults of ev'ry sinful dame:
You still may prattle nor give o'er,
When wretched I must sin no more.
The sprightly Nine must leave me then,
This trembling hand resign its pen;
No matron ever sweetly sung,
Apollo only courts the young;
And who would not, Aurelia, pray,   40
Enjoy his favours while they may?
Nor cramp nor head-ache shall prevail;
I'll still write on, and you shall rail.

The Sacrifice: An Epistle to Celia*

If you, dear Celia, cannot bear,
The low delights that others share:
If nothing will your palate fit
But learning, eloquence and wit,
Why, you may sit alone (I ween)
Till you're devoured with the spleen:
But if variety can please
With humble scenes and careless ease;
If smiles can banish melancholy,
Or whimsy with its parent folly;   10
If any joy in these there be,
I dare invite you down to me.
    You know these little roofs of mine
Are always sacred to the Nine;
This day we make a sacrifice
To the Parnassian deities,
Which I am ordered by Apollo,
To show you in the words that follow.
    As first we purge the hallowed room
With soft utensil called a broom;   20
And next for you a throne prepare,
Which vulgar mortals call a chair,
While zephyrs from an engine blow,
And bid the sparkling cinders glow;
Then gather round the mounting flames,
The priestess and assembled dames,
While some inferior maid shall bring
Clear water from the bubbling spring:
Shut up in vase of sable dye,
Secure from each unhallowed eye,   30
Fine wheaten bread you next behold,
Like that which Homer sings of old,
And by some unpolluted fair
It must be scorched with wond'rous care:
So far 'tis done: And now behold

146

The sacred vessels – not of gold:
Of polished earth must they be formed,
With painting curiously adorned;
These rites are past: And now must follow
The grand libation to Apollo,   40
Of juices drawn from magic weeds,
And pith of certain Indian reeds.
For flow'r of milk the priestess calls,
Her voice re-echoes from the walls;
With hers the sister voices blend,
And with the od'rous steam ascend:
Each fair one now a sibyl grows,
And ev'ry cheek with ardour glows.
And (though not quite beside their wits)
Are seized with deep prophetic fits: 50
Some by mysterious figures show
That Celia loves a shallow Beau;
And some by signs and hints declare
That Damon will not wed Ziphair:
Their neighbours' fortunes each can tell,
So potent is the mighty spell.

   This is the feast and this, my friend,
Are you commanded to attend:
Yes at your peril: But adieu,
I've tired both myself and you.   60

On Winter
(In imitation of an Epistle by Ambrose Philips)

What pictures now shall wanton fancy bring?
Or how the Muse to Artemisia sing?
Now shiv'ring Nature mourns her ravished charms,
And sinks supine in winter's frozen arms.
No gaudy banks delight the ravished eye,

But northern breezes whistle through the sky.
No joyful choirs hail the rising day,
But the froze crystal wraps the leafless spray:
Brown look the meadows, that were late so fine,
And capped with ice the distant mountains shine;   10
The silent linnet views the gloomy sky,
Skulks to his hawthorn, nor attempts to fly:
The heavy clouds send down the feathered snow;
Through naked trees the hollow tempests blow;
The shepherd sighs, but not his sighs prevail;
To the soft snow succeeds the rushing hail;
And these white prospects soon resign their room
To melting showers and unpleasing gloom;
The nymphs and swains their aching fingers blow,
Shun the cold rains and bless the kinder snow;   20
While the faint travellers around them see,
Here seas of mud and there a leafless tree:
No budding leaves nor honeysuckles gay,
No yellow crow-foots paint the dirty way;
The lark sits mournful as afraid to rise,
And the sad finch his softer song denies.

Poor daggled Urs'la stalks from cow to cow,
Who to her sighs return a mournful low;
While their full udders her broad hands assail,
And her sharp nose hangs dropping o'er the pail.   30
With garments trickling like a shallow spring,
And his wet locks all twisted in a string,
Afflicted Cymon waddles through the mire,
And rails at Winifred creeping o'er the fire.

Say gentle Muses, say, is this a time
To sport with poesy and laugh in rhyme;
While the chilled blood, that hath forgot to glide,
Steals through its channels in a lazy tide:
And how can Phoebus, who the Muse refines,
Smooth the dull numbers when he seldom shines.   40

Mira's Will*

IMPRIMIS – My departed shade I trust
To heav'n – My body to the silent dust;
My name to public censure I submit,
To be disposed of as the world thinks fit;
My vice and folly let oblivion close,
The world already is o'erstocked with those;
My wit I give, as misers give their store,
To those that think they had enough before.
Bestow my patience to compose the lives
Of slighted virgins and neglected wives;   10
To modish lovers I resign my truth,
My cool reflection to unthinking youth;
And some good-nature give ('tis my desire)
To surly husbands, as their needs require;
And first discharge my funeral – and then
To the small poets I bequeath my pen.
    Let a small sprig (true emblem of my rhyme)
Of blasted laurel on my hearse recline;
Let some grave wight, that struggles for renown
By chanting dirges through a market-town,   20
With gentle step precede the solemn train;
A broken flute upon his arm shall lean.
Six comic poets shall the corse surround,
And all free-holders, if they can be found:
Then follow next the melancholy throng,
As shrewd instructors, who themselves are wrong.
The virtuoso, rich in sun-dried weeds,
The politician, whom no mortal heeds,
The silent lawyer, chambered all the day,
And the stern soldier that receives no pay.   30
But stay – the mourners should be first our care:
Let the freed 'prentice lead the miser's heir;
Let the young relict wipe her mournful eye,
And widowed husbands o'er their garlic cry.
    All this let my executors fulfil,

And rest assured that this is Mira's will,
Who was, when she these legacies designed,
In body healthy, and composed in mind.

MARY JONES
d.1778

Daughter of Oliver Jones of Oxford, and sister of Revd Oliver Jones, Chanter of Christ Church Cathedral, Oxford. Despite her modest social position and financial circumstances (she was probably a governess) had several aristocratic friends. Friend of Dr Johnson, who used to quote *Il Penseroso* at her: 'Chauntress oft the woods among, I woo...'; Thomas Warton said, 'She was a very ingenious poetess...and, on the whole, was a most sensible, agreeable, and amiable woman'. Her volume of poems lists some 1,504 subscribers, beginning with the Prince of Orange and ranging through Christopher Smart, Horace Walpole, David Garrick, and well-nigh innumerable aristocrats, dons, clergymen, lawyers and Joneses.

Miscellanies in Prose and Verse (Oxford, 1750).

from *An Epistle to Lady Bowyer**

How much of paper's spoiled! what floods of ink!
And yet how few, how very few can think!
The knack of writing is an easy trade;
But to think well requires – at least a head.
Once in an age, *one* genius may arise,
With wit well-cultured, and with learning wise.
Like some tall oak, behold his branches shoot!
No tender scions springing at the root.
While lofty Pope erects his laurelled head,
No lays, like mine, can live beneath his shade.   10
Nothing but weeds, and moss, and shrubs are found.
Cut, cut them down, why cumber they the ground?

And yet you'd have me write! – For what? for whom?
To curl a fav'rite in a dressing-room?
To mend a candle when the snuff's too short?
Or save rappee for chamber-maids at Court?
Glorious ambition! noble thirst of fame! –

No, but you'd have me write – to get a name.
Alas! I'd live unknown, unenvied too;
'Tis more than Pope, with all his wit can do.   20
'Tis more than you, with wit and beauty joined,
A pleasing form, and a discerning mind.
The world and I are no such cordial friends;
I have my purpose, they their various ends.
I say my prayers, and lead a sober life,
Nor laugh at Cornus, or at Cornus' wife.
What's fame to me, who pray, and pay my rent?
If my friends know me honest, I'm content.
   Well, but the joy to see my works in print!
My self too pictured in a mezzo-tint!   30
The Preface done, the Dedication framed,
With lies enough to make a Lord ashamed!
Thus I step forth; an auth'ress in some sort.
My patron's name? 'O choose some Lord at Court.
'One that has money which he dares not use,
'One you may flatter much, that is, abuse.
'For if you're nice, and cannot change your note,
'Regardless of the trimmed, or untrimmed coat;
'Believe me, friend, you'll ne'er be worth a groat.' [. . .]
   Well then, to cut this mighty matter short,   40
I've neither friend, nor interest at Court.
Quite from St. James's to thy stairs, Whitehall,
I hardly know a creature, great or small,
Except one Maid of Honour, worth 'em all.
I have no business there. Let those attend
The courtly Levee, or the courtly friend,
Who more than fate allows them, dare to spend.
Or those whose avarice, with much, craves more,
The pensioned beggar, or the titled poor.
These are the thriving breed, the tiny great!   50
Slaves! wretched slaves! the journeymen of State!
Philosophers! who calmly bear disgrace,
Patriots! who sell their country for a place! [. . .]

After the Small Pox

When skilful traders first set up,
To draw the people to their shop,
They straight hang out some gaudy sign,
Expressive of the goods within.
The vintner has his boy and grapes,
The haberdasher thread and tapes,
The shoemaker exposes boots,
And Monmouth Street old tattered fruits.

    So fares it with the nymph divine;
For what is beauty but a sign?   10
A face hung out, through which is seen
The nature of the goods within.
    Thus the coquet her beau ensnares
With studied smiles, and forward airs;
The graver prude hangs out a frown
To strike th'audacious gazer down;
But she alone, whose temp'rate wit
Each nicer medium can hit,
Is still adorned with ev'ry grace,
And wears a sample in her face.   20

What though some envious folks have said,
That Stella now must hide her head,
That all her stock of beauty's gone,
And ev'n the very sign took down:
Yet grieve not at the fatal blow;
For if you break a while, we know,
'Tis bankrupt like, more rich to grow.
A fairer sign you'll soon hang up,
And with fresh credit open shop:
For nature's pencil soon shall trace,   30
And once more finish off your face,
Which all your neighbours shall out-shine,
And of your mind remain the sign.

Soliloquy on an empty Purse

Alas! my Purse! how lean and low!
My silken purse! what art thou now!
Once I beheld – but stocks will fall –
When both thy ends had wherewithal.
When I within thy slender fence
My fortune placed, and confidence;
A poet's fortune! – not immense:
Yet mixed with keys, and coins among,
Chinked to the melody of song.

Canst thou forget when, high in air,   10
I saw thee flutt'ring at a fair?
And took thee, destined to be sold,
My lawful purse, to have and hold?
Yet used so often disembogue,
No prudence could thy fate prorogue.
Like wax thy silver melted down,
Touch but the brass, and lo! 'twas gone:
And gold would never with thee stay,
For gold had wings, and flew away.

Alas, my purse! yet still be proud,   20
For see the virtues round thee crowd!
See, in the room of paltry wealth,
Calm temp'rance rise, the nurse of health;
And self-denial, slim and spare,
And fortitude, with look severe;
And abstinence, to leanness prone,
And patience, worn to skin and bone:
Prudence, and foresight on thee wait,
And poverty lies here in state!
Hopeless her spirits to recruit,   30
For ev'ry virtue is a mute.

Well then, my purse, thy sabbath keep;
Now thou art empty, I shall sleep.
No silver sounds shall thee molest,
Nor golden dreams disturb my breast.
Safe shall I walk the streets along,
Amidst temptations thick and strong,
Catched by the eye, no more shall stop
At Wildey's toys, or Pinchbeck's shop;
Nor, cheap'ning Payne's ungodly books,   40
Be drawn aside by pastry cooks:
But fearless now we both may go
Where Ludgate's mercers bow so low;
Beholding all with equal eye,
Nor moved at – 'Madam, what d'ye buy?'
Away, far hence each worldly care!
Nor dun, nor pick-purse shalt thou fear,
Nor flatt'rer base annoy my ear.
Snug shalt thou travel through the mob,
For who a poet's purse will rob?   50
And softly sweet, in garret high,
Will I thy virtues magnify,
Out-soaring flatt'rers' stinking breath,
And gently rhyming rats to death.

ANNA LAETITIA BARBAULD
1743-1825

Born in Leicestershire, the eldest child of Jane (Jennings) and John Aikin, a prominent Nonconformist clergyman and schoolteacher, who encouraged her education. Her first volume appeared in 1773; next year she married Revd Rochemont Barbauld, of Huguenot stock, with whom she set up a school (though she declined to set up a college for young ladies, as being unsuitable for their sex); after some years' instability, he died insane in 1808. She had many literary acquaintances, including members of the Bluestocking circle; entered into public debate, supporting Wilberforce and the Slavery Abolition Bill; published devotional pieces, and essays on Akenside and Collins, edited Richardson's letters, and collections of British Novelists (in fifty volumes). Her writing is manifestly sensible, imaginative and good-humoured.

Poems (London, 1773); *The Works of Anna Laetitia Barbauld, with a Memoir by Lucy Aikin*, 2 vols (London: Longman, 1825); Betsy Rodgers, *Georgian Chronicle: Mrs. Barbauld and her Family* (London: Methuen, 1968).

On a Lady's Writing

Her even lines her steady temper show,
Neat as her dress, and polished as her brow;
Strong as her judgement, easy as her air;
Correct though free, and regular though fair:
And the same graces o'er her pen preside,
That form her manners and her footsteps guide.

Tomorrow

See where the falling day
In silence steals away
Behind the western hills withdrawn:
Her fires are quenched, her beauty fled,
While blushes all her face o'erspread

156

As conscious she had ill fulfilled
The promise of the dawn.

Another morning soon shall rise,
Another day salute our eyes,
As smiling and as fair as she,   10
And make as many promises:
But do not thou
The tale believe,
They're sisters all,
And all deceive.

Washing-Day*

> ...and their voice
> Turning again towards childish treble, pipes
> And whistles in its sound...

The Muses are turned gossips; they have lost
The buskined step, and clear high-sounding phrase,
Language of gods. Come then, domestic Muse,
In slipshod measure loosely prattling on
Of farm or orchard, pleasant curds and cream,
Or drowning flies, or shoe lost in the mire
By little whimpering boy, with rueful face;
Come, Muse, and sing the dreaded Washing-Day.
Ye who beneath the yoke of wedlock bend,
With bowed soul, full well ye ken the day   10
Which week, smooth sliding after week, brings on
Too soon; – for to that day nor peace belongs
Nor comfort; – ere the first grey streak of dawn,
The red-armed washers come and chase repose.
Nor pleasant smile, nor quaint device of mirth,
E'er visited that day: the very cat,
From the wet kitchen scared and reeking hearth,
Visits the parlour, – an unwonted guest.

The silent breakfast-meal is soon despatched;
Uninterrupted, save by anxious looks   20
Cast at the lowering sky, if sky should lower.
From that last evil, O preserve us heavens!
For should the skies pour down, adieu to all
Remains of quiet: then expect to hear
Of sad disasters, – dirt and gravel stains
Hard to efface, and loaded lines at once
Snapped short, – and linen-horse by dog thrown down,
And all the petty miseries of life.
Saints have been calm while stretched upon the rack,
And Guatimozin smiled on burning coals;   30
But never yet did housewife notable
Greet with a smile a rainy washing-day.
– But grant the welkin fair, require not thou
Who call'st thyself perchance the master there,
Or study swept, or nicely dusted coat,
Or usual 'tendance; – ask not, indiscreet,
Thy stockings mended, though the yawning rents
Gape wide as Erebus; nor hope to find
Some snug recess impervious; shouldst thou try
The 'customed garden walks, thine eye shall rue   40
The budding fragrance of thy tender shrubs,
Myrtle or rose, all crushed beneath the weight
Of coarse checked apron, – with impatient hand
Twitched off when showers impend: or crossing lines
Shall mar thy musings, as the wet cold sheet
Flaps in thy face abrupt. Woe to the friend
Whose evil stars have urged him forth to claim
On such a day the hospitable rites!
Looks, blank at best, and stinted courtesy,
Shall he receive. Vainly he feeds his hopes   50
With dinner of roast chicken, savoury pie,
Or tart or pudding: – pudding he nor tart
That day shall eat; nor, though the husband try,
Mending what can't be helped, to kindle mirth
From cheer deficient, shall his consort's brow

Clear up propitious: – the unlucky guest
In silence dines, and early slinks away.
I well remember, when a child, the awe
This day struck into me; for then the maids,
I scarce knew why, looked cross, and drove me from them;   60
Nor soft caress could I obtain, nor hope
Usual indulgencies; jelly or creams,
Relic of costly suppers, and set by
For me their petted one; or buttered toast,
When butter was forbid; or thrilling tale
Of ghost or witch, or murder – so I went
And sheltered me beside the parlour fire:
There my dear grandmother, eldest of forms,
Tended the little ones, and watched from harm,
Anxiously fond, though oft her spectacles   70
With elfin cunning hid, and oft the pins
Drawn from her ravelled stocking, might have soured
One less indulgent. –
At intervals my mother's voice was heard,
Urging dispatch: briskly the work went on,
All hands employed to wash, to rinse, to wring,
To fold, and starch, and clap, and iron, and plait.
Then would I sit me down, and ponder much
Why washings were. Sometimes through hollow bowl
Of pipe amused we blew, and sent aloft   80
The floating bubbles; little dreaming then
To see, Montgolfier, thy silken ball
Ride buoyant through the clouds – so near approach
The sports of children and the toils of men.
Earth, air, and sky, and ocean, hath its bubbles,
And verse is one of them – this most of all.

The Rights of Woman*

Yes, injured Woman! rise, assert thy right!
Woman! too long degraded, scorned, oppressed;

159

O born to rule in partial Law's despite,
Resume thy native empire o'er the breast!

Go forth arrayed in panoply divine,
That angel pureness which admits no stain;
Go, bid proud Man his boasted rule resign
And kiss the golden sceptre of thy reign.

Go, gird thyself with grace, collect thy store
Of bright artillery glancing from afar;   10
Soft melting tones thy thundering cannon's roar,
Blushes and fears thy magazines of war.

Thy rights are empire: urge no meaner claim, –
Felt, not defined, and if debated, lost;
Like sacred mysteries, which withheld from fame,
Shunning discussion are revered the most.

Try all that wit and art suggest to bend
Of thy imperial foe the stubborn knee;
Make treacherous Man thy subject, not thy friend;
Thou mayst command, but never canst be free.   20

Awe the licentious and restrain the rude;
Soften the sullen, clear the cloudy brow:
Be, more than princes' gifts, thy favours sued; –
She hazards all, who will the least allow.

But hope not, courted idol of mankind,
On this proud eminence secure to stay;
Subduing and subdued, thou soon shalt find
Thy coldness soften, and thy pride give way.

Then then abandon each ambitious thought;
Conquest or rule thy heart shall feebly move,   30
In Nature's school, by her soft maxims taught
That separate rights are lost in mutual love.

ANNA SEWARD
1742-1809

Known as 'the Swan of Lichfield', she was probably the most praised woman poet of her time. Born in Derbyshire, eldest child of Revd Thomas Seward, later Canon at Lichfield, and Elizabeth (Hunter), daughter of the headmaster of Lichfield School. Several poems express her affection for, and grief at the early death of her adopted sister, Honora Sneyd; never married, despite various proposals; a friend of the 'Ladies of Llangollen' (her volume, *Llangollen Vale, with Other Poems*, published 1796); poems also appeared in the *Batheaston Miscellany* of Lady Anna Riggs Miller (satirized in *Pickwick Papers* as authoress of 'Ode to an Expiring Frog'). Her poetry on public themes expresses liberal, patriotic values, while she also elaborated (the right word for her style) elegiac themes, especially on young women.

Walter Scott (ed.), *The Poetical Works of Anna Seward*, 3 vols (Edinburgh and London, 1810); Hesketh Pearson, *The Swan of Lichfield* (London: Hamish Hamilton, 1936); Ruth Avaline Hesselgrave, *Lady Miller and the Batheaston Literary Circle* (New Haven: Yale UP, 1927).

Verses
Inviting Mrs. C— to Tea on a public Fast-day During the American War*

Dear Stella, 'mid the pious sorrow
Our monarch bids us feel to-morrow,
The ahs! and ohs! supremely triste,
The abstinence from beef, and whist;
Wisely ordained to please the Lord,
And force him whet our edgeless sword,
Till, shipping o'er the Atlantic rill,
We cut provincial throats at will;
'Midst all the penitence we feel
For merry sins, –'midst all the zeal   10
For vengeance on the saucy foe,
Who lays our boasted legions low;

I wish, when sullen evening comes,
That you, to gild its falling glooms,
Would, without scruple cold, agree
Beneath these walls to sip your tea.
From the chaste, fragrant, Indian weed
Our sins no pampering juices feed;
And though the hours, with contrite faces,
May banish the ungodly aces,   20
And take of food a sparing bit,
They'll gluttonize on Stella's wit.

'Tea!' cries a Patriot, 'on that day
'Twere good you flung the drug away,
Rememb'ring 'twas the cruel source
Of sad distrust, and long divorce
'Twixt nations, which, combined, had hurled
Their conquering javelin round the world.

'O! Indian shrub, thy fragrant flowers
To England's weal had deadly powers,   30
When Despotism, with impious hand,
To venom turned thy essence bland,
To venom, subtle, foul and fell,
As steeped the dart of Isdabel!

'Have we forgot the dread libation
Which cost the life of half the nation?
When Boston, with indignant thought
Saw poison in the perfumed draught,
And caused her troubled bay to be
But one vast bowl, of bitter tea;   40
While Ate, chiefly bidden guest,
Came sternly to the fatal feast,
And mingled with its baneful flood
Brothers'! – children's! – parents' blood;
Dire as the banquet Atreus served,
When his own son Thyestes carved,

And Phoebus, shrinking from the sight,
Drew o'er his orb the pall of night.

'Tomorrow then, at least, refrain,
Nor quaff thy bleeding country's bane!   50
For O! reflect, poetic daughter,
'Twas hapless Britain's laurel-water'.

from *Colebrook Dale**
[The Industrial Revolution's effect on the Midlands]

Scene of superfluous grace, and wasted bloom,
O, violated COLEBROOK! [. . .]
                        . . . What though to vulgar eye
Invisible, yet oft the lucid gaze
Of the rapt Bard, in every dell and glade
Beheld them wander, – saw, from the clear wave
Emerging, all the wat'ry sisters rise,
Wearing the aqueous lily, and the flag,
In wreaths fantastic, for the tresses bright
Of amber-haired Sabrina. – Now we view   10
Their fresh, their fragrant, and their silent reign
Usurped by Cyclops; – hear, in mingled tones,
Shout their thronged barge, their pond'rous engines clang
Through thy coy dales; while red the countless fires,
With umbered flames, bicker on all thy hills,
Dark'ning the summer's sun with columns large
Of thick, sulphureous smoke, which spread, like palls,
That screen the dead, upon the sylvan robe
Of thy aspiring rocks; pollute thy gales,
And stain thy glassy waters – see, in troops,   20
The dusk artificers, with brazen throats,
Swarm on thy cliffs, and clamour in thy glens,
Steepy and wild, ill suited to such guests [. . .]
    While neighbouring cities waste the fleeting hours,
Careless of art and knowledge and the smile

Of every Muse, expanding Birmingham,
Illumed by intellect, as gay in wealth,
Commands her aye-accumulating walls
From month to month to climb the adjacent hills,
Creep on the circling plains, now here, now there,   30
Divergent – change the hedges, thickets, trees,
Upturned, disrooted, into mortared piles,
The streets elongate and the statelier square [. . .]
. . . Warned by the Muse, if Birmingham should draw,
In future years, from more congenial climes
Her massy ore, her labouring sons recall,
And sylvan Colebrook's winding vales restore
To beauty and to song, content to draw
From unpoetic scenes her rattling stores,
Massy and dun; if, thence supplied, she fail,   40
Britain, to glut thy rage commercial, see
Grim Wolverhampton lights her smouldering fires,
And Sheffield's smoke-involved; dim where she stands
Circled by lofty mountains, which condense
Her dark and spiral wreaths to drizzling rains,
Frequent and sullied, as the neighbouring hills
Ope their deep veins and feed her caverned flames;
While to her dusky sister Ketley yields,
From her long-desolate and livid breast,
The ponderous metal. No aerial forms   50
On Sheffield's arid moor or Ketley's heath
E'er wove the floral crowns, or smiling stretched
The shelly sceptre; – there no poet roved
To catch bright inspirations. Blush, ah, blush,
Thou venal Genius of these outraged groves,
And thy apostate head with thy soiled wings
Veil! – who hast thy beauteous charge resigned
To habitants ill-suited; hast allowed
Their rattling forges and their hammers' din,
And hoarse, rude throats, to fright the gentle train,   60
Dryads and fair-haired Naiades; – the song,
Once loud as sweet, of the wild woodland choir

164

To silence; – disenchant the poet's spell,
And to a gloomy Erebus transform
The destined rival of Tempean vales.

Invocation, To the Genius of Slumber
Written Oct. 1787*

Spirit of dreams, that when the dark hours steep
In the soft dews of life-enbalming sleep,
Our busy senses, canst restore the lost,
The loved, the mourned, from Death's mysterious coast,
Propitious lately to my votive lay,
And the lone musings of the joyless day,
From 'whelming years, and from sepulchral night,
Thou gav'st HONORA to my slumbering sight:
Decked in those various graces that arrayed
In youth's first bloom, the fair ingenuous maid,   10
In all those pure affection's gladd'ning powers,
That winged for joy the animated hours,
Alike when her sweet converse welcome made
Morn's rising light, and evening's stealthy shade;
The months with flowers adorned, with radiance warm
The vernal day, and e'en the wintry storm.
She looked, as in those golden years foregone,
Spoke, as when love attuned each melting tone,
When, by my side, her cautious steps she moved,
Watching the friend solicitously loved,   20
Whose youthful strength, in one disastrous day,
Had fall'n to luckless accident a prey,
And needed much, to save from future harm,
The eye attentive, the supporting arm.
Remembered looks, ye rays of friendship's flame,
Long my soul's light, and guardians of my frame!

Why, visionary power, so seldom kind
To the deprived, the life-retracing mind;

Withholding oft, 'mid thy obtrusive swarm,
My day-dream's idol, fair Honora's form?   30
O! when thou giv'st it, then, and only then,
Lost to my woes, I live with her again.
Again on me those soft'ning eye-balls shine!
I hear her speak! I feel her arm on mine!
Real as fair, the tender pleasures glow,
Sweet, as the past was potent to bestow,
Freed from that sense which shrouds with dire control
Volition's image in a cypress stole;
That tells me, searching wide creation o'er,
My dear Honora I shall find no more;   40
That on her lonely grave, and mouldering form,
Six dreary winters poured the ruthless storm,
Violent and dark as my soul's primal woe
When first I found that beauteous head laid low.
On that unshrined, yet ever-sacred spot,
By faithless Love deserted and forgot,
Six bloomy springs their crystal light have showed,
Their sun-gilt rains in fragrant silence flowed,
Mild as my sorrows (calmed by passing years),
Time-softened sighs, and time-assuaged tears.   50

Once, as the taper's steady light conveyed
Upon the white expanse the graceful shade
Of sweet Honora's face, the traces fair
My anxious hand pursued, and fixed them there,
To throw, in spite of Fate's remorseless crimes,
Soft sooting magic o'er succeeding times.
For this dear purpose, near my couch I placed
The shade, by Love assiduously traced;
And, while no sullen curtain drops between,
The image consecrates the sombrous scene;   60
Serenely sweet it stands, – at morn, at eve,
The first, last object these fond eyes perceive,
And still my heart, and oft my lips address
The shadowy form of her who lived to bless.

Now strikes the midnight clock; – the taper gleams
With the faint flash of half-expiring beams,
And soon that lovely semblance shall recede,
And Sleep's dim veils its thrilling powers impede.
I feel their balmy, kind, resistless charms
Creep o'er my closing eyes, – I fold my arms,   70
Breathing in murmurs through the paly gloom,
'Come to my dreams, my lost Honora, come!
Back as the waves of Time benignly roll,
Show thy bright face to my enchanted soul!'

HANNAH MORE
1745-1833

The fourth of five daughters of a charity-school master, Jacob More; well-educated, within the limits he felt appropriate to women's more delicate brains; the older sisters ran a successful school in Bristol. About 1767 began a long engagement, which fell through in 1773. Began visiting London, and entered into literary society, becoming one of the Bluestocking group. In 1784 helped the Bristol milkwoman poet, Anne Yearsley, but later they quarrelled. Established Sunday-schools for the poor, campaigned against the slave trade, and wrote large quantities of didactic works and conservative propaganda (*The Riot* is impressive in its insolence). Was very popular, and extremely successful financially, skilfully combining the conservatively moralistic with the entertaining. In her pastoral dialogue *Florella*, Urania argues,

> So Woman born to dignify retreat,
> Unknown to flourish, and unseen be great,
> To give domestic life its sweetest charm...
> Should seek but Heaven's applauses, and her own.

Of Mary Wollstonecraft, she remarked, 'Rights of women! We will be hearing of the Rights of Children next!'

Poems (London, 1816); *Works*, 6 vols (London, 1834); Mary G. Jones, *Hannah More* (Cambridge: CUP, 1952); Walter Sidney Scott, *The Blue Stocking Ladies* (London: John Green, 1947).

from *The Bas Bleu; Or, Conversation**
[An account of Blue-Stocking parties]

> ... Long was Society o'er-run
> By whist, that desolating Hun;
> Long did quadrille despotic sit,
> That Vandal of colloquial wit;
> And conversation's setting light
> Lay half-obscured in Gothic night.
> At length the mental shades decline,
> Colloquial wit begins to shine;
> Genius prevails, and conversation

Emerges into Reformation [. . .]   **10**
   Hail, Conversation, soothing power,
Sweet goddess of the social hour!
O may thy worship long prevail,
And thy true votaries never fail!
Long may thy polished altars blaze
With wax-lights' undiminished rays!
Still be thy nightly offerings paid,
Libations large of lemonade!
In silver vases, loaded, rise
The biscuits' ample sacrifice!   **20**
Nor be the milk-white streams forgot
Of thirst-assuaging, cool orgeat;
Rise, incense pure from fragrant tea,
Delicious incense, worthy thee! [. . .]
   Enlightened spirits! you, who know
What charms from polished converse flow,
Speak, for you can, the pure delight
When kindling sympathies unite;
When correspondent tastes impart
Communion sweet from heart to heart [. . .]   **30**
   In taste, in learning, wit or science,
Still kindred souls demand alliance;
Each in the other joys to find
The image answering to his mind.
But sparks electric only strike
On souls electrical alike;
The flash of intellect expires,
Unless it meet congenial fires:
The language to th'elect alone
Is, like the Masons' mystery, known;   **40**
In vain th'unerring sign is made
To him who is not of the Trade.
What lively pleasure to divine
The thought implied, the hinted line,
To feel allusion's artful force,
And trace the image to its source!

Quick memory blends her scattered rays,
Till fancy kindles at the blaze;
The works of ages starts to view,
And ancient wit elicits new.   50

    But wit and parts if thus we praise,
What nobler altars should we raise,
Those sacrifices could we see
Which wit, o virtue! makes to thee.
At once the rising thought to dash,
To quench at once the bursting flash!
The shining mischief to subdue,
And lose the praise and pleasure too! [...]
Blush, heroes, at your cheap renown,
A vanquished realm, a plundered town!   60
Your conquests were to gain a name,
This conquest triumphs over fame;
So pure its essence, 'twere destroyed
If known, and if commended, void.

The Riot; or Half a Loaf is Better than No Bread
In a Dialogue between Jack Anvil and Tom Hod*

'Come, neighbours, no longer be patient and quiet,
Come let us go kick up a bit of a riot;
I am hungry, my lads, but I've little to eat,
So we'll pull down the mills and seize all the meat:
I'll give you good sport, boys, as ever you saw,
So a fig for the justice, a fig for the law.'

Then his pitchfork Tom seized – 'Hold a moment,' says Jack,
'I'll show thee thy blunder, brave boy, in a crack.
And if I don't prove we had better be still,
I'll assist thee straightway to pull down every mill;   10
I'll show thee how passion thy reason does cheat,
Or I'll join thee in plunder for bread and for meat.

170

'What a whimsy to think thus our bellies to fill,
For we stop all the grinding by breaking the mill!
What a whimsy to think we shall get more to eat
By abusing the butchers who get us the meat!
What a whimsy to think we shall mend our spare diet
By breeding disturbance, by murder and riot!

'Because I am dry, 'twould be foolish, I think,
To pull out my tap and to spill all my drink;   20
Because I am hungry and want to be fed,
That is sure no wise reason for wasting my bread;
And just such wise reasons for mending their diet
Are used by those blockheads who rush into riot.

'I would not take comfort for others' distresses,
But still I would mark how God our land blesses;
For though in Old England the times are but sad,
Abroad I am told they are ten times as bad;
In the land of the Pope there is scarce any grain,
And 'tis still worse, they say, both in Holland and Spain.   30

'Let us look to the harvest our wants to beguile,
See the lands with rich crops how they everywhere smile!
Meantime to assist us, by each western breeze,
Some corn is brought daily across the salt seas.
We'll drink little tea, no whisky at all,
But patiently wait and the prices will fall.

'But if we're not quiet, then let us not wonder
If things grow much worse by our riot and plunder;
And let us remember, whenever we meet,
The more ale we drink, boys, the less we shall eat.   40
On those days spent in riot, *no* bread you brought home:
Had you spent them in labour, you might have had *some*.

'A dinner of herbs, says the wise man, with quiet
Is better than beef amid discord and riot.
If the thing can't be helped, I'm a foe to all strife,
And pray for a peace every night of my life;
But in matters of state not an inch will I budge,
Because I conceive I'm no very good judge.

'But though poor, I can work, my brave boy, with the best,
Let the King and the Parliament manage the rest;   50
I lament both the war and the taxes together,
Though I verily think they don't alter the weather.
The King, as I take it with very good reason,
May prevent a bad law but can't help a bad season.

'The Parliament-men, although great is their power,
Yet they cannot contrive us a bit of a shower;
And I never yet heard, though our rulers are wise,
That they know very well how to manage the skies;
For the best of them all, as they found to their cost,
Were not able to hinder last winter's hard frost.   60

'Besides, I must share in the wants of the times,
Because I have had my full share in its crimes;
And I'm apt to believe the distress which is sent
Is to punish and cure us of all discontent.
But harvest is coming – potatoes will come!
Our prospect clears up. Ye complainers be dumb!

'And though I've no money and though I've no lands,
I've a head on my shoulders and a pair of good hands;
So I'll work the whole day and on Sundays I'll seek
At church how to bear all the wants of the week.   70
The gentlefolks too will afford us supplies;
They'll subscribe – and they'll give up their puddings and pies.

'Then before I'm induced to take part in a riot,
I'll ask this short question – What shall I get by it?
So I'll e'en want a little till cheaper the bread,
For a mittimus hangs o'er each rioter's head;
And when of two evils I'm asked which is best,
I'd rather be hungry than hanged, I protest.'

Quoth Tom, 'Thou art right; if I rise, I'm a Turk',
So he threw down his pitchfork and went to his work.   80

CHARLOTTE SMITH
1749-1806

Her mother Anna (Towers) died when she was three; the impending remarriage of her father, Nicholas Turner, a landed gentleman of Sussex, when she was fifteen, provoked her into marrying Benjamin Smith, son of a West India merchant, who recklessly wasted their money and brought them to debtors' prison. Her tenth child was born in 1785, but in 1784 she also produced her *Elegiac Sonnets* (eleven editions by 1851), marked by the raptures, anguish and bad weather of the Gothick sensibility. After leaving her husband, supported herself and her children by novel-writing (averaging a book a year for twenty years). The mode is generally Gothick, Mr Smith modelling for a series of bad husbands; the later novels were thought too politically liberal. Her *Beachy Head* volume displays a lively interest in nature, wry humour, and a romantic yearning for lost innocence.

Elegiac Sonnets (London, 1784); *Beachy Head, with Other Poems* (London, 1807); Florence May Hilbish, *Charlotte Smith, Poet and Novelist* (Hughesville, Penn., 1941); Katharine M. Rogers, *Feminism in Eighteenth Century England* (Brighton: Harvester, 1982).

Written in the churchyard at Middleton in Sussex

Pressed by the moon, mute arbitress of tides,
　　While the loud equinox its power combines,
　　The sea no more its swelling surge confines,
But o'er the shrinking land sublimely rides.
The wild blast, rising from the western cave,
　　Drives the huge billows from their heaving bed,
　　Tears from their grassy tombs the village dead,
And breaks the silent sabbath of the grave!
With shells and seaweed mingled, on the shore
　　Lo! their bones whiten in the frequent wave;　　　　10
　　But vain to them the winds and waters rave;
They hear the warring elements no more:
While I am doomed – by life's long storm oppressed,
To gaze with envy on their gloomy rest.

On the Aphorism: 'L'Amitié est l'amour sans ailes'

Friendship, as some sage poet sings,
Is chastened Love, deprived of wings,
Without all wish or power to wander;
Less volatile, but not less tender:
Yet says the proverb – 'Sly and slow
'Love creeps, even where he cannot go;'
To clip his pinions then is vain,
His old propensities remain;
And she, whose years *beyond fifteen*,
Has counted *twenty*, may have seen   10
How rarely unplumed Love will stay;
He flies not – but he coolly walks away.

from *Beachy Head*

... *I* once was happy, when while yet a child,
I learned to love these upland solitudes,
And, when elastic as the mountain air,
To my light spirit, care was yet unknown
And evil unforeseen: – Early it came,
And childhood scarcely passed, I was condemned,
A guiltless exile, silently to sigh,
While Memory, with faithful pencil, drew
The contrast [...]
An early worshipper at Nature's shrine,   10
I loved her rudest scenes – warrens, and heaths,
And yellow commons, and birch-shaded hollows,
And hedge rows, bordering unfrequented lanes
Bowered with wild roses, and the clasping woodbine
Where purple tassels of the tangling vetch
With bittersweet, and bryony inweave,
And the dew fills the silver bindweed's cups –
I loved to trace the brooks whose humid banks
Nourish the harebell, and the freckled pagil;

175

And stroll among o'ershadowing woods of beech,   20
Lending in summer, from the heats of noon
A whispering shade; while haply there reclines
Some pensive lover of uncultured flowers,
Who, from the tumps with bright green mosses clad,
Plucks the wood sorrel, with its light thin leaves,
Heart-shaped, and triply folded; and its root
Creeping like beaded coral; or who there
Gathers, the copse's pride, anemones,
With rays like golden studs on ivory laid
Most delicate; but touched with purple clouds,   30
Fit crown for April's fair but changeful brow.

Ah! hills so early loved! in fancy still
I breathe your pure keen air; and still behold
Those widely spreading views, mocking alike
The poet and the painter's utmost art.
The visionary, nursing dreams like these,
Is not indeed unhappy. Summer woods
Wave over him, and whisper as they wave [. . .]

Thirty-eight: Addressed to Mrs H—y*

In early youth's unclouded scene,
The brilliant morning of eighteen,
With health and sprightly joy elate
    We gazed on life's enchanting spring,
    Nor thought how quickly time would bring
The mournful period – Thirty-eight.

Then the starch maid or matron sage,
Already of that sober age,
We viewed with mingled scorn and hate,
    In whose sharp words or sharper face   10
    With thoughtless mirth we loved to trace
The sad effects of – Thirty-eight.

Till saddening, sickening at the view,
We learned to dread what time might do;
And then preferred a prayer to fate
    To end our days ere that arrived,
    When (power and pleasure long survived)
We met neglect and – Thirty-eight.

But time, in spite of wishes, flies,
And fate our simple prayer denies,   20
And bids us death's own hour await:
    The auburn locks are mixed with grey,
    The transient roses fade away,
But reason comes at – Thirty-eight.

Her voice the anguish contradicts
That dying vanity inflicts;
Her hand new pleasures can create.
    For us she opens to the view
    Prospects less bright – but far more true,
And bids us smile at – Thirty-eight.   30

No more shall scandal's breath destroy
The social converse we enjoy
With bard or critic tete a tete;
    O'er youth's bright blooms her blights shall pour,
    But spare the improving friendly hour
That science gives to – Thirty-eight.

Stripped of their gaudy hues by truth,
We view the glitt'ring toys of youth,
And blush to think how poor the bait
    For which to public scenes we ran   40
    And scorned of sober sense the plan
Which gives content at – Thirty-eight.

Though time's inexorable sway
Has torn the myrtle bands away,
For other wreaths 'tis not too late;
   The amaranth's purple glow survives
   And still Minerva's olive lives
On the calm brow of – Thirty-eight.

With eye more steady we engage
To contemplate approaching age,   50
And life more justly estimate.
   With firmer souls and stronger powers,
   With reason, faith and friendship ours,
   We'll not regret the stealing hours
That lead from Thirty – even to Forty-eight.

DOROTHY WORDSWORTH
1771-1855

'Her eyes were not soft, as Mrs. Wordsworth's, nor were they fierce or bold; but they were wild and startling, and hurried in their motion. Her manner was warm and even ardent; her sensibility seemed constitutionally deep; and some subtle fire of impassioned intellect apparently burned within her, which, being alternately pushed forward into a conspicuous expression by the irrepressible instincts of her temperament, and then immediately checked, in obedience to the decorum of her sex and age, and her maidenly condition, gave to her whole demeanour, and to her conversation, an air of embarrassment, and even self-conflict, that was most distressing to witness' (Thomas De Quincey). Born in Cockermouth, third child and only daughter of Ann and John Wordsworth, land agent, one year after William. After her mother's death when she was six, was brought up by relatives, but set up home with William in 1795, moving to Dove Cottage, Grasmere, in 1797. Her sensitively-written journals recount their life together and her response to the natural world. Was very distressed at William's marriage; contracted a near-fatal fever in 1829; from 1835 to her death, frequently insane. Little she wrote was published in her lifetime. 'During the last years of her life her poetry was paramount. She copied and recopied her verses; she recited them continually... Most obviously, her poems exist intertextually with those of her brother... The poetic presence of her brother made it difficult for Dorothy to write poetry' (Levin).

Susan M. Levin, *Dorothy Wordsworth and Romanticism* (New Brunswick and London: Rutgers State UP, 1987), includes the poems; Robert Gittings and Jo Manton, *Dorothy Wordsworth* (Oxford: Clarendon, 1985); Margaret Homans, *Women Writers and Poetic Identity* (Princeton: Princeton UP, 1980).

Grasmere – a Fragment

Peaceful our valley, fair and green,
And beautiful her cottages,
Each in its nook, its sheltered hold,
Or underneath its tuft of trees

Many and beautiful they are;
But there is *one* that I love best,
A lowly shed, in truth, it is,
A brother of the rest.

Yet when I sit on rock or hill,
Down looking on the valley fair,   10
That cottage with its clustering trees
Summons my heart; it settles there.

Others there are whose small domain
Of fertile fields and hedgerows green
Might more seduce a wanderer's mind
To wish that *there* his home had been.

Such wish be his! I blame him not,
My fancies they perchance are wild
– I love that house because it is
The very mountains' child.   20

Fields hath it of its own, green fields,
But they are rocky steep and bare;
Their fence is of the mountain stone,
And moss and lichen flourish there.

And when the storm comes from the north
It lingers near that pastoral spot,
And, piping through the mossy walls,
It seems delighted with its lot.

And let it take its own delight;
And let it range the pastures bare;   30
Until it reach that group of trees,
– It may not enter there!

A green unfading grove it is,
Skirted with many a lesser tree,
Hazel and holly, beech and oak,
A bright and flourishing company.

Precious the shelter of those trees;
They screen the cottage that I love;
The sunshine pierces to the roof,
And the tall pine-trees tower above.   **40**

When first I saw that dear abode,
It was a lovely winter's day:
After a night of perilous storm
The west wind ruled with gentle sway;

A day so mild, it might have been
The first day of the gladsome spring;
The robins warbled, and I heard
One solitary throstle sing.

A stranger, Grasmere, in thy vale,
All faces then to me unknown,   **50**
I left my sole companion-friend
To wander out alone.

Lured by a little winding path,
I quitted soon the public road,
A smooth and tempting path it was,
By sheep and shepherds trod.

Eastward, toward the lofty hills,
This pathway led me on
Until I reached a stately rock,
With velvet moss o'ergrown.   **60**

With russet oak and tufts of fern
Its top was richly garlanded;
Its sides adorned with eglantine
Bedropped with hips of glossy red.

There, too, in many a sheltered chink
The foxglove's broad leaves flourished fair,
And silver birch whose purple twigs
Bend to the softest breathing air.

Beneath that rock my course I stayed,
And, looking to its summit high,   70
'Thou wear'st,' said I, 'a splendid garb,
Here winter keeps his revelry.'

'Full long a dweller on the plains,
I grieved when summer days were gone;
No more I'll grieve; for winter here
Hath pleasure gardens of his own.

What need of flowers? The splendid moss
Is gayer than an April mead;
More rich its hues of various green,
Orange, and gold, and glittering red.'   80

—Beside that gay and lovely rock
There came with merry voice
A foaming streamlet glancing by;
It seemed to say 'Rejoice!'

My youthful wishes all fulfilled,
Wishes matured by thoughtful choice,
I stood an inmate of this vale
How *could* I but rejoice?

Floating Island at Hawkshead,
An Incident in the schemes of Nature

Harmonious powers with Nature work
On sky, earth, river, lake, and sea:
Sunshine and storm, whirlwind and breeze
All in one duteous task agree.

Once did I see a slip of earth,
By throbbing waves long undermined,
Loosed from its hold; – *how* no one knew
But all might see it float, obedient to the wind.

Might see it, from the verdant shore
Dissevered float upon the lake,   10
Float, with its crest of trees adorned
On which the warbling birds their pastime take.

Food, shelter, safety there they find
There berries ripen, flowerets bloom;
There insects live their lives – and die:
A peopled *world* it is; – in size a tiny room.

And thus through many seasons' space
This little island may survive
But Nature, though we mark her not,
Will take away – may cease to give.   20

Perchance when you are wandering forth
Upon some vacant sunny day
Without an object, hope, or fear,
Thither your eyes may turn – the isle is passed away.

Buried beneath the glittering lake!
Its place no longer to be found,
Yet the lost fragments shall remain,
To fertilize some other ground.

Thoughts on my sick-bed

And has the remnant of my life
Been pilfered of this sunny spring?
And have its own prelusive sounds
Touched in my heart no echoing string?

Ah! say not so – the hidden life
Couchant within this feeble frame
Hath been enriched by kindred gifts,
That, undesired, unsought-for, came

With joyful heart in youthful days
When fresh each season in its round   10
I welcomed the earliest celandine
Glittering upon the mossy ground

With busy eyes I pierced the lane
In quest of known and *un*known things,
– The primrose a lamp on its fortress rock,
The silent butterfly spreading its wings,

The violet betrayed by its noiseless breath,
The daffodil dancing in the breeze,
The carolling thrush, on his naked perch,
Towering above the naked trees.   20

Our cottage-hearth no longer our home,
Companions of Nature were we,
The stirring, the still, the loquacious, the mute –
To all we gave our sympathy.

Yet never in those careless days
When spring-time in rock, field, or bower
Was but a fountain of earthly hope
A promise of fruits and the *splendid* flower.

No! then I never felt a bliss
That might with *that* compare   30
Which, piercing to my couch of rest,
Came on the vernal air.

When loving friends an offering brought,
The first flowers of the year,
Culled from the precincts of our home,
From nooks to memory dear.

With some sad thoughts the work was done,
Unprompted and unbidden,
But joy it brought to my *hidden* life,
To consciousness no longer hidden.   40

I felt a power unfelt before,
Controlling weakness, languor, pain;
It bore me to the terrace walk
I trod the hills again; –

No prisoner in this lonely room,
I *saw* the green banks of the Wye,
Recalling thy prophetic words,
Bard, brother, friend from infancy!

No need of motion, or of strength,
Or even the breathing air: 50
–I thought of Nature's loveliest scenes;
And with memory I was there.

JANE TAYLOR
1783-1824

Her father was Isaac Taylor, of Ongar, an engraver who became a Non-conformist minister in Colchester; her elder sister, Ann Gilbert, was also a successful writer. From 1812, lived with her brother; wrote mostly children's and religious verse ('Twinkle, twinkle, little star'), but frequently displays a dry humour and social observation.

Essays in Rhyme, on Morals and Manners (London, 1816).

*Recreation**

'– We took our work, and went, you see,
To take an early cup of tea.
We did so now and then, to pay
The friendly debt, and so did they.
Not that our friendship burnt so bright
That all the world could see the light;
'Twas of the ordinary *genus*,
And little love was lost between us;
We loved, I think, about as true,
As such near neighbours mostly do.   10

At first, we all were somewhat dry; –
Mamma felt cold, and so did I:
Indeed, that room, sit where you will,
Has draught enough to turn a mill.
"I hope you're warm," says Mrs. G.
"O, quite so," says mamma, *says she*;
"I'll take my shawl off by and by." –
"This room is always warm," says I.

At last the tea came up, and so,
With that, our tongues began to go.   20
Now, in that house you're sure of knowing
The smallest scrap of news that's going;

186

We find it *there* the wisest way,
To take some care of what we say.

–Says she, "There's dreadful doings still
In that affair about the *will*;
For now the folks in Brewer's Street,
Don't speak to James's, when they meet.
Poor Mrs. Sam sits all alone,
And frets herself to skin and bone.   30
For months she managed, she declares,
All the old gentleman's affairs;
And always let him have his way,
And never left him night nor day;
Waited and watched his every look,
And gave him every drop he took.
Dear Mrs. Sam, it was too bad!
He might have left her all he had."

"Pray ma'am," says I, "has poor Miss A.
Been left as *handsome* as they say?"   40
"My dear," says she, "'tis no such thing,
She'd nothing but a mourning ring.
But is it not *uncommon* mean
To wear that rusty bombazine!"
"She had," says I, "the very same,
Three years ago, for – what's his name?" –
"The Duke of Brunswick, – very true,
And has not bought a thread of new,
I'm positive," said Mrs. G. –
So then we laughed, and drank our tea.   50

   "So," says mamma, "I find it's true
What Captain P. intends to do;
To hire that house, or else to buy –"
"Close to the tan-yard, ma'am," says I;
"Upon my word it's very strange,
I wish they mayn't repent the change!"

187

"My dear," says she, "'tis very well
You know, if *they* can bear the smell."

"Miss F.," says I, "is said to be
A sweet young woman, Mrs. G."   60
"O, excellent! I hear," she cried;
"O, truly so!" mamma replied.
"How old should you suppose her, pray?
She's older than she looks, they say."
"Really," says I, "she seems to me
Not more than twenty-two or three."
"O, then you're wrong," says Mrs. G.
"Their upper servant told our Jane,
She'll not see twenty-nine again."
"Indeed, so old! I wonder why   70
She does not marry, then," says I;
"So many thousands to bestow,
And such a beauty, too, you know."
"A beauty! O, my dear Miss B.
You must be joking, now," says she;
"Her *figure*'s rather pretty," – "Ah!
That's what *I* say," replied mamma.

"Miss F.," says I, "I've understood,
Spends all her time in doing good:
The people say her coming down   80
Is quite a blessing to the town."
At that our hostess fetched a sigh,
And shook her head; and so, says I,
"It's very kind of her, I'm sure,
To be so generous to the poor".
"No doubt," says she, "'tis very true;
Perhaps there may be *reasons* too: –
You know some people like to pass
For *patrons* with the lower class."
And here I break my story's thread,   90
Just to remark, that what she said,

188

Although I took the other part,
Went like a cordial to my heart.

Some innuendos more had passed,
Till out the scandal came at last.
"Come then, I'll tell you something more,"
Says she, – "Eliza, shut the door. –
I would not trust a creature here,
For all the world, but you, my dear.
Perhaps it's false – I hope it may,
– But let it go no farther, pray!"
"O," says mamma, "You need not fear,
We never mention what we hear."
"Indeed we shall not, Mrs. G."
Says I, again, impatiently:
And so we drew our chairs the nearer,
And whispering, lest the child should hear her,
She told a tale, at least too *long*,
To be repeated in a song;
We, panting every breath between,
With curiosity and spleen.
And how we did enjoy the sport!
And echo every faint report,
And answer every candid doubt,
And turn her motives inside out,
And holes in all her virtues pick,
Till we were sated, almost sick.

– Thus having brought it to a close,
In great good humour, we arose.
Indeed, 'twas more than time to go,
Our boy had been an hour below.
So, warmly pressing Mrs. G.
To fix a day to come to tea,
We muffled up in cloak and plaid,
And trotted home behind the lad.'

The Squire's Pew

A slanting ray of evening light
   Shoots through the yellow pane;
It makes the faded crimson bright,
   And gilds the fringe again:
The window's gothic frame-work falls
In oblique shadow on the walls.

How since these trappings first were new,
   How many a cloudless day,
To rob the velvet of its hue,
   Has come and passed away!   10
How many a setting sun has made
That curious lattice-work of shade!

Crumbled beneath the hillock green,
   The cunning hand must be,
That carved this fretted door, I ween,
   Acorn, and *fleur-de-lis*;
And now the worm hath done her part,
In mimicking the chisel's art.

In days of yore (as now we call)
   When the first James was king;   20
The courtly knight from yonder hall,
   Hither his train did bring;
All seated round in order due,
With broidered suit and buckled shoe.

On damask cushions, set in fringe,
   All reverently they knelt:
Prayer-books, with brazen hasp and hinge,
   In ancient English spelt,
Each holding in a lily hand,
Responsive at the priest's command.   30

—Now, streaming down the vaulted aisle,
    The sunbeam, long and lone,
Illumes the characters awhile
    Of their inscription stone;
And there, in marble hard and cold,
The knight and all his train behold.

Outstretched together, are expressed
    He and my lady fair;
With hands uplifted on the breast,
    In attitudes of prayer;   40
Long visaged, clad in armour, he,
With ruffled arm and bodice, she.

Set forth, in order as they died,
    The numerous offspring bend;
Devoutly kneeling side by side,
    As though they did intend
For past omissions to atone,
By saying endless prayers in stone.

Those mellow days are past and dim
    But generations new,   50
In regular descent from him,
    Have filled the stately pew;
And in the same succession go,
To occupy the vault below.

And now, the polished, modern squire,
    And his gay train appear;
Who duly to the hall retire,
    A season, every year;
And fill the seats with belle and beau,
As 'twas so many years ago.   60

Perchance, all thoughtless as they tread
   The hollow sounding floor,
Of that dark house of kindred dead,
   Which shall, as heretofore,
In turn, receive, to silent rest,
Another, and another guest.

The feathered hearse and sable train,
   In all its wonted state,
Shall wind along the village lane,
   And stand before the gate;   70
—Brought many a distant county through
To join the final rendez-vous.

And when the race is swept away,
   All to their dusty beds;
Still shall the mellow evening ray
   Shine gaily o'er their heads:
While other faces, fresh and new,
Shall occupy the squire's pew.

FELICIA DOROTHEA HEMANS
1793-1835

> She met the tempest, meekly brave,
> Then turn'd o'erwearied to the grave.

Perhaps the most popular woman poet throughout the century. 'The Homes of England' has now effectively disappeared into Noel Coward's exuberant parody – 'The stately homes of England, / How beautiful they stand, / To prove the upper classes / Have still the upper hand...' Born Felicia Dorothea Browne, in Liverpool, fifth child of a successful Irish merchant. In 1807 her first volume of poems was printed; in 1812 married an army officer, Captain Hemans, by whom she had five sons before he left her in 1818. Wrote profusely, over a wide range, dealing with Biblical and historical material (Byron derided her writings on Greece); William Rossetti later criticized her poetry for its 'cloying flow of right-minded perceptions of moral and material beauty'. An exponent of the developing Victorian myth of the pure, long-suffering woman, her *Records of Woman* provided a series of moral-sentimental stories of virtuous female suffering.

Works of Felicia Dorothea Hemans (London, 1839).

The Homes of England

The stately homes of England,
   How beautiful they stand,
Amidst their tall ancestral trees,
   O'er all the pleasant land!
The deer across their greensward bound,
   Through shade and sunny gleam;
And the swan glides past them with the sound
   Of some rejoicing stream.

The merry homes of England!
   Around their hearths by night,   10
What gladsome looks of household love
   Meet in the ruddy light!

There woman's voice flows forth in song,
  Or childhood's tale is told,
Or lips move tunefully along
  Some glorious page of old.

The blessed homes of England!
  How softly on their bowers
Is laid the holy quietness
  That breathes from Sabbath hours!   20
Solemn, yet sweet, the church-bell's chime
  Floats through their woods at morn;
All other sounds, in that still time,
  Of breeze and leaf are born.

The cottage homes of England!
  By thousands on her plains,
They are smiling o'er the silvery brooks,
  And round the hamlet fanes.
Through glowing orchards forth they peep,
  Each from its nook of leaves;   30
And fearless there the lowly sleep,
  As the bird beneath their eaves.

The free fair homes of England!
  Long, long in hut and hall,
May hearts of native proof be reared
  To guard each hallowed wall!
And green for ever be the groves,
  And bright the flowery sod,
Where first the child's glad spirit loves
  Its country and its God!

The Indian Woman's Death Song

Down a broad river of the western wilds,
Piercing thick forest-glooms, a light canoe
Swept with the current: fearful was the speed
Of the frail bark, as by a tempest's wing
Borne leaf-like on to where the mist of spray
Rose with the cataract's thunder. Yet within,
Proudly, and dauntlessly, and all alone,
Save that a babe lay sleeping at her breast,
A woman stood! Upon her Indian brow
Sat a strange gladness, and her dark hair waved   10
As if triumphantly. She pressed her child,
In its bright slumber, to her beating heart,
And lifted her sweet voice, that rose awhile
Above the sound of waters, high and clear,
Wafting a wild proud strain – a song of death.

'Roll swiftly to the spirits' land, thou mighty stream and free!
Father of ancient waters, roll! and bear our lives with thee!
The weary bird that storms have tossed would seek the sunshine's
    calm,
And the deer that hath the arrow's hurt flies to the woods of balm.

'Roll on! – my warrior's eye hath looked upon another's face,   20
And mine hath faded from his soul, as fades a moonbeam's trace:
My shadow comes not o'er his path, my whisper to his dream –
He flings away the broken reed. Roll swifter yet, thou stream!

'The voice that spoke of other days is hushed within *his* breast,
But *mine* its lonely music haunts, and will not let me rest;
It sings a low and mournful song of gladness that is gone –
I cannot live without that light. Father of waves! roll on!

'Will he not miss the bounding step that met him from the chase?
The heart of love that made his home an ever-sunny place?   [30
The hand that spread the hunter's board, and decked his couch of
      yore? –
He will not! Roll, dark foaming stream, on to the better shore!

'Some blessed fount amidst the woods of that bright land must
      flow,
Whose water from my soul may lave the memory of this woe;
Some gentle wind must whisper there, whose breath may waft
      away
The burden of the heavy night, the sadness of the day.

'And thou, my babe! though born, like me, for woman's weary lot,
Smile! – to that wasting of the heart, my own! I leave thee not;
Too bright a thing art *thou* to pine in aching love away –
Thy mother bears thee far, young fawn! from sorrow and decay.

She bears thee to the glorious bowers where none are heard   40
      to weep,
And where th'unkind one hath no power again to trouble sleep;
And where the soul shall find its youth, as wakening from a dream:
One moment, and that realm is ours. On, on, dark-rolling stream!'

ELIZABETH BARRETT BROWNING
1806-1861

'One of those rare writers who risk themselves adventurously and disinterestedly in an imaginative life' (Virginia Woolf). Eldest of eleven children of Mary Graham Clarke and Edward Moulton Barrett, whose wealth derived from Jamaican sugar plantations; he encouraged her warmly, publishing her *Battle of Marathon* in 1820. From childhood suffered from pulmonary troubles (possibly partly psychosomatic), becoming a persistent invalid, reclining in a darkened room. Father was notoriously possessive; her *Poems* of 1844 brought an admiring letter from Robert Browning ('I love your verses with all my heart, dear Miss Barrett'); after a secret courtship, they eloped and married in 1846 (her father never forgave her). Settled in Florence; in 1849 bore a son; in 1851 published *Casa Guidi Windows* on the Italian Risorgimento, and in 1856 her verse novel, *Aurora Leigh*, a *succès de scandale*, a romance on the role of woman and the problems of the poet; in her later years developed spiritualist tastes. At one time she was proposed as Poet Laureate, but her reputation collapsed by the end of the century; a revival seems under way.

The Poetical Works of Elizabeth Barrett Browning (London: OUP, 1910); Virginia Woolf, *The Common Reader, Second Series* (London: Hogarth, 1932); Alethea Hayter, *Mrs. Browning. A Poet's Work and Its Setting* (London: Faber; NY: Barnes and Noble, 1963); Peter Dally, *Elizabeth Barrett Browning: A Psychological Portrait* (London: Macmillan, 1989).

from *Sonnets from the Portuguese**

V

I lift my heavy heart up solemnly,
As once Electra her sepulchral urn,
And, looking in thine eyes, I overturn
The ashes at thy feet. Behold and see
What a great heap of grief lay hid in me,
And how the red wild sparkles dimly burn
Through the ashen greyness. If thy foot in scorn
Could tread them out to darkness utterly,
It might be well perhaps. But if instead

Thou wait beside me for the wind to blow   10
The grey dust up, ... those laurels on thy head,
O my Beloved, will not shield thee so,
That none of all the fires shall scorch and shred
The hair beneath. Stand farther off then! go.

                              XXIX
I think of thee! – my thoughts do twine and bud
About thee, as wild vines, about a tree,
Put out broad leaves, and soon there's nought to see
Except the straggling green which hides the wood.
Yet, O my palm-tree, be it understood
I will not have my thoughts instead of thee
Who art dearer, better! Rather, instantly
Renew thy presence; as a strong tree should,
Rustle thy boughs and set thy trunk all bare,
And let those bands of greenery which insphere thee
Drop heavily down, – burst, shattered, everywhere!
Because, in this deep joy to see and hear thee
And breathe within thy shadow a new air,
I do not think of thee – I am too near thee.

                *To George Sand: A Recognition**

True genius, but true woman! dost deny
Thy woman's nature with a manly scorn,
And break away the gauds and armlets worn
By weaker women in captivity?
Ah, vain denial! that revolted cry
Is sobbed in by a woman's voice forlorn! –
Thy woman's hair, my sister, all unshorn,
Floats back dishevelled strength in agony,
Disproving thy man's name! and while before
The world thou burnest in a poet-fire,   10
We see thy woman-heart beat evermore

                              198

Through the large flame. Beat purer, heart, and higher,
Till God unsex thee on the heavenly shore,
Where unincarnate spirits purely aspire.

from *Casa Guidi Windows**

from PART I

I heard last night a little child go singing
   'Neath Casa Guidi windows, by the church,
O bella libertà, O bella! – stringing
   The same words still on notes he went in search
So high for, you concluded the upspringing
   Of such a nimble bird to sky from perch
Must leave the whole bush in a tremble green,
   And that the heart of Italy must beat,
While such a voice had leave to rise serene
   'Twixt church and palace of a Florence street: 10
A little child, too, who not long had been
   By mother's finger steadied on his feet,
And still *O bella libertà* he sang [...]

from PART II

Long live the people! How they lived! and boiled
And bubbled in the cauldron of the street:
   How the young blustered, nor the old recoiled,
And what a thunderous stir of tongues and feet
   Trod flat the palpitating bells and foiled
The joy-guns of their echo, shattering it!
   How down they pulled the Duke's arms everywhere!
How up they set new cafe-signs, to show
   Where patriots might sip ices in pure air –
(The fresh paint smelling somewhat)! To and fro   10
   How marched the Civil Guard, and stopped to stare
When boys broke windows in a civic glow!
   How rebel songs were sung to loyal tunes,

And bishops cursed in ecclesiastic metres [. . .]
. . . How all the nobles fled, and would not wait,
    Because they were most noble, – which being so,
How Liberals vowed to burn their palaces,
    Because free Tuscans were not free to go!
How grown men raged at Austria's wickedness,
    And smoked, – while fifty striplings in a row   20
Marched straight to Piedmont for the wrong's redress!
    You say we failed in duty, we who wore
Black velvet like Italian democrats,
    Who slashed our sleeves like patriots, nor forswore
The true republic in the form of hats?
    We chased the archbishop from the Duomo door,
We chalked the walls with bloody caveats
    Against all tyrants. If we did not fight
Exactly, we fired muskets up the air
    To show that victory was ours of right.   30
We met, had free discussion everywhere
    (Except perhaps i' the Chambers) day and night.
We proved the poor should be employed, . . . that's fair, –
    And yet the rich not worked for anywise, –
Pay certified, yet prayers abrogated, –
    Full work secured, yet liabilities
To overwork excluded, – not one bated
    Of all our holidays, that still, at twice
Or thrice a week, are moderately rated [. . .]

from *Aurora Leigh*

from FIRST BOOK: YOUNG AURORA'S FOSTERMOTHER
I think I see my father's sister stand
Upon the hall-step of her country-house
To give me welcome. She stood straight and calm,
Her somewhat narrow forehead braided tight
As if for taming accidental thoughts
From possible pulses; brown hair pricked with grey

By frigid use of life (she was not old,
Although my father's elder by a year),
A nose drawn sharply, yet in delicate lines;
A close mild mouth, a little soured about   10
The ends, through speaking unrequited loves
Or peradventure niggardly half-truths;
Eyes of no colour, – once they might have smiled,
But never, never have forgot themselves
In smiling; cheeks, in which was yet a rose
Of perished summers, like a rose in a book,
Kept more for ruth than pleasure, – if past bloom,
Past fading also.
                    She had lived, we'll say,
A harmless life, she called a virtuous life,   20
A quiet life, which was not life at all
(But that, she had not lived enough to know),
Between the vicar and the country squires,
The lord-lieutenant looking down sometimes
From the empyrean to assure their souls
Against chance vulgarisms, and, in the abyss,
The apothecary, looked on once a year
To prove the soundness of humility.
The poor-club exercised her Christian gifts
Of knitting stockings, stitching petticoats,   30
Because we are of one flesh, after all,
And need one flannel (with a proper sense
Of difference in the quality) – and still
The book-club, guarded from your modern trick
Of shaking dangerous questions from the cream,
Preserved her intellectual. She had lived
A sort of cage-bird life, born in a cage,
Accounting that to leap from perch to perch
Was act and joy enough for any bird.
Dear heaven, how silly are the things that live   40
In thickets, and eat berries!
                    I, alas,
A wild bird scarcely fledged, was brought to her cage,

And she was there to meet me. Very kind.
Bring the clean water, give out the fresh seed. [. . .]

from FIFTH BOOK
Nay, if there's room for poets in this world
A little overgrown (I think there is),
Their sole work is to represent the age,
Their age, not Charlemagne's, – this live, throbbing age,
That brawls, cheats, maddens, calculates, aspires,
And spends more passion, more heroic heat,
Betwixt the mirrors of its drawing-rooms,
Than Roland with his knights at Roncesvalles.
To flinch from modern varnish, coat or flounce,
Cry out for togas and the picturesque,   10
Is fatal, – foolish too. King Arthur's self
Was commonplace to Lady Guenever;
And Camelot to minstrels seemed as flat
As Fleet Street to our poets.
                                        Never flinch,
But still, unscrupulously epic, catch
Upon the burning lava of a song
The full-veined, heaving, double-breasted Age:
That, when the next shall come, the men of that
May touch the impress with reverent hand, and say   20
'Behold, – behold the paps we all have sucked!
This bosom seems to beat still, or at least
It sets ours beating: this is living art,
Which thus presents and thus records true life.'

What form is best for poems? Let me think
Of forms less, and the external. Trust the spirit,
As sovran nature does, to make the form;
For otherwise we only imprison spirit
And not embody. Inward evermore
To outward, – so in life, and so in art   30
Which still is life [. . .]

A Musical Instrument

I

What was he doing, the great god Pan,
   Down in the reeds by the river?
Spreading ruin and scattering ban,
Splashing and paddling with hoofs of a goat,
And breaking the golden lilies afloat
   With the dragon-fly on the river.

II

He tore out a reed, the great god Pan,
   From the deep cool bed of the river:
The limpid water turbidly ran,
And the broken lilies a-dying lay,   10
And the dragon-fly had fled away,
   Ere he brought it out of the river.

III

High on the shore sate the great god Pan,
   While turbidly flowed the river;
And hacked and hewed as a great god can,
With his hard bleak steel at the patient reed,
Till there was not a sign of a leaf indeed
   To prove it fresh from the river.

IV

He cut it short, did the great god Pan
   (How tall it stood in the river!),   20
Then drew the pith, like the heart of a man,
Steadily from the outside ring,
And notched the poor dry empty thing
   In holes, as he sate by the river.

V

'This is the way,' laughed the great god Pan
    (Laughed while he sate by the river),
'The only way, since gods began
To make sweet music, they could succeed.'
Then, dropping his mouth to a hole in the reed,
    He blew in power by the river.   30

VI

Sweet, sweet, sweet, O Pan!
    Piercing sweet by the river!
Blinding sweet, O great god Pan!
The sun on the hill forgot to die,
And the lilies revived, and the dragon-fly
    Came back to dream on the river.

VII

Yet half a beast is the great god Pan,
    To laugh as he sits by the river,
Making a poet out of a man:
The true gods sigh for the cost and the pain, –   40
For the reed which grows nevermore again
    As a reed with the reeds in the river.

THE BRONTË SISTERS

Although grouped together here, they do not constitute some triple-headed monster, the Brontësaurus, but display marked individualities. Very important as Romantic novelists, they are not negligible as poets. Generally they share a Gothick-Romantic sensibility of emotional extremism, exploring imagination, liberty and solitude, in verse of some technical limitation (verse-forms deriving from hymns and ballads, with somewhat repetitive vocabulary and ideas). Respectively the third, fifth and sixth children of Revd Patrick Brontë and Maria Branwell (d.1821) of Thornton, Yorkshire, they were educated mostly at home in Haworth, where they wrote profusely. In 1831, Charlotte began teaching, and in 1842 went with Emily to Belgium, where she fell unhappily in love with the school proprietor's husband; returned in 1846. In that year published, with her sisters, *Poems by Currer, Ellis and Acton Bell* (two copies sold); in 1847, *Jane Eyre*; in 1848, brother Branwell and Emily died, in 1849, Anne. In 1854, married father's curate Arthur Bell Nicholls, and died nine months later. Emily, the most notably passionate and violent nature, wrote copiously from an early age; she and Anne occupied themselves with prose (now lost) and verse fantasies on the imaginary realm of Gondal. Despite brief teaching experiences away, lived mostly at home; most of her poems written 1844-6; *Wuthering Heights* published 1847; died of tuberculosis. Anne, the least forceful of the three, was not happy away from home; possible romance with father's curate; *Agnes Grey* published 1847; poems remarkable for general extreme misery, for some of which Calvinism was responsible.

A selection: E. Chitham and T. Winnifrith (eds.), *Selected Brontë Poems* (Oxford: Blackwell, 1985); C.W. Hatfield (ed.), *The Complete Poems of Emily Jane Brontë* (NY: Columbia UP, 1941); E. Chitham (ed.), *The Poems of Anne Brontë* (London: Macmillan, 1979); Edith Gaskell, *The Life of Charlotte Brontë* (London, 1857); T. Winnifrith, *The Brontës and their background: romance and reality* (London: Macmillan, 1973).

CHARLOTTE BRONTË
1816-1855

'Again I find myself alone'

Again I find myself alone, and ever
  The same voice like an oracle begins
Its vague and mystic strain, forgetting never
  Reproaches for a hundred hidden sins,
And setting mournful penances in sight,
Terrors and tears for many a watchful night.

Fast change the scenes upon me all the same,
  In hue and drift the regions of a land
Peopled with phantoms, and how dark their aim
  As each dim guest lifts up its shadowy hand   10
And parts its veil to show one withering look,
That mortal eye may scarce unblighted brook.

I try to find a pleasant path to guide
  To fairer scenes – but still they end in gloom;
The wilderness will open dark and wide
  As the sole vista to a vale of bloom,
Of rose and elm and verdure – as these fade
Their sere leaves fall on yonder sandy shade.

My dreams, the Gods of my religion, linger
  In foreign lands, each sundered from his own,   20
And there has passed a cold destroying finger
  O'er every image, and each sacred tone
Sounds low and at a distance, sometimes dying
Like an uncertain sob, or smothered sighing.

Sea-locked, a cliff surrounded, or afar
  Asleep upon a fountain's marble brim –
Asleep in heart, though yonder early star,
  The first that lit its taper soft and dim

By the great shrine of heaven, has fixed its eye
Unsmiling though unsealed on that blue sky.   30

Left by the sun, as he is left by hope:
   Bowed in dark, placid cloudlessness above,
As silent as the Island's palmy slope,
   All beach untrodden, all unpeopled grove,
A spot to catch each moonbeam as it smiled
Towards that thankless deep so wide and wild.

Thankless he too looks up, no grateful bliss
   Stirs him to feel the twilight-breeze diffuse
Its balm that bears in every spicy kiss
   The mingled breath of southern flowers and dews,   40
Cool and delicious as the fountain's spray
Showered on the shining pavement where he lay.

'What does she dream of'

What does she dream of, lingering all alone
   On the vast terrace, o'er the stream impending?
Through all the still, dim night no life-like tone
   With the soft rush of wind and wave is blending.
Her fairy step upon the marble falls
With startling echo through those silent halls.

Chill is the night, though glorious, and she folds
   Her robe upon her breast to meet that blast
Coming down from the barren Northern wolds.
   There, how she shuddered as the breeze blew past   10
And died on yonder track of foam, with shiver
Of giant reed and flag fringing the river.

Full, brilliant shines the moon – lifted on high
   O'er noble land and nobler river flowing,
Through parting hills that swell upon that sky
   Still with the hue of dying daylight glowing,

Swell with their plumy woods and dewy glades,
Opening to moonlight in the deepest shades.

Turn, lady, to thy halls, for singing shrill
  Again the gust descends – again the river   20
Frets into foam – I see thy dark eyes fill
  With large and bitter tears – thy sweet lips quiver.

Diving

Look into thought and say what thou dost see;
  Dive be not fearful how dark the waves flow;
Sing through the surge, and bring pearls up to me;
  Deeper, ay, deeper; the fairest lie low.

'I have dived, I have sought them, but none have I found;
  In the gloom that closed o'er me no form floated by;
As I sank through the void depths, so black and profound,
  How dim died the sun and how far hung the sky.'

'What had I given to hear the soft sweep
  Of a breeze bearing life through that vast realm of death!   10
Thoughts were untroubled and dreams were asleep:
  The spirit lay dreadless and hopeless beneath.'

from *Retrospection*

   ... Dream that stole o'er us in the time
   When life was in its vernal clime,
   Dream that still faster o'er us steals
     As the mild star of spring declining
   The advent of that day reveals,
     That glows in Sirius' fiery shining:
   Oh! as thou swellest, and as the scenes
     Cover this cold world's darkest features,

Stronger each change my spirit weans
   To bow before thy god-like creatures.   10

When I sat 'neath a strange roof-tree
With naught I knew or loved round me,
Oh how my heart shrank back to thee,
Then I felt how fast thy ties had bound me.

That hour, that bleak hour when the day
   Closed in the cold autumn's gloaming,
When the clouds hung so bleak and drear and grey
   And a bitter wind through their folds was roaming,
There shone no fire on the cheerless hearth,
   In the chamber there gleamed no taper's twinkle.   20
Within, neither sight nor sound of mirth,
   Without, but the blast, and the sleet's chill sprinkle.

Then sadly I longed for my own dear home
   For a sight of the old familiar faces,
I drew near the casement and sat in its gloom
   And looked forth on the tempest's desolate traces.

Ever anon that wolfish breeze
   The dead leaves and sere from their boughs was shaking,
And I gazed on the hills through the leafless trees
   And felt as if my heart was breaking.   30

Where was I ere an hour had passed:
Still listening to that dreary blast,
Still in that mirthless lifeless room,
Cramped, chilled and deadened by its gloom?

No! thanks to that bright darling dream,
Its power had shot one kindling gleam,
Its voice had sent one wakening cry,
And bade me lay my sorrows by,
And called me earnestly to come,
And borne me to my moorland home.   40

I heard no more the senseless sound
Of task and chat that hummed around,
I saw no more that grisly night
Closing the day's sepulchral sight.

The vision's spell had deepened o'er me:
Its lands, its scenes were spread before me,
In one short hour a hundred homes
Had roofed me with their lordly domes,
And I had sat by fires whose light
Flashed wide o'er halls of regal height,   50
And I had seen them come and go
Whose forms gave radiance to that glow,
And I had heard the matted floor
Of ante-room and corridor
Shake to some half-remembered tread
Whose haughty firmness woke even dread,
As through the curtained portal strode
Some spurred and fur-wrapped Demi-God,
Whose ride through that tempestuous night
   Had added somewhat of a frown   60
To brows that shadowed eyes of light
   Fit to flash fire from Scythian crown,
Till sweet salute from lady gay
Chased that unconscious scowl away;
And then the savage fur-cap doffed,
   The Georgian mantle laid aside,
The satrap stretched on cushion soft,
   His loved and chosen by his side,
That hand, that in its horseman's glove
   Looked fit for naught but bridle rein,   70
Caresses now its lady-love
   With fingers white that show no strain
They got in hot and jarring strife,
When hate or honour warred with life, –
Naught redder than the roseate ring
That glitters fit for Eastern King [. . .]

EMILY BRONTË
1818-1848

'High waving heather'

High waving heather 'neath stormy blasts bending,
Midnight and moonlight and bright shining stars,
Darkness and glory rejoicingly blending,
Earth rising to heaven and heaven descending,
Man's spirit away from its drear dungeon sending,
Bursting the fetters and breaking the bars.

All down the mountain sides wild forests lending
One mighty voice to the life-giving wind,
Rivers their banks in the jubilee rending,
Fast through the valleys a reckless course wending,   10
Wider and deeper their waters extending,
Leaving a desolate desert behind.

Shining and lowering and swelling and dying,
Changing forever from midnight to noon;
Roaring like thunder, like soft music sighing,
Shadows on shadows advancing and flying,
Lightning-bright flashes the deep gloom defying,
Coming as swiftly and fading as soon.

Plead for Me

O, thy bright eyes must answer now,
When Reason, with a scornful brow,
Is mocking at my overthrow;
O, thy sweet tongue must plead for me
And tell why I have chosen thee!

Stern Reason is to judgement come
Arrayed in all her forms of gloom;
Wilt thou my advocate be dumb?
No, radiant angel, speak and say
Why I did cast the world away:					10

Why I have persevered to shun
The common paths that others run
And on a strange road journeyed on;
Heedless alike of wealth and power –
Of Glory's wealth and Pleasure's flower.

These once indeed seemed beings divine
And they perchance heard vows of mine
And saw my offerings on their shrine –
But, careless gifts are seldom prized
And mine were worthily despised.					20

So with a ready heart I swore
To seek their altar-stone no more,
And gave my spirit to adore
Thee, ever present phantom thing,
My Slave, my Comrade, and my King!

A Slave because I rule thee still,
Incline thee to my changeful will
And make thy influence good or ill –
A Comrade – for by day and night
Thou art my Intimate Delight –					30

My darling pain that wounds and sears
And wrings a blessing out from tears
By deadening me to earthly cares;
And yet a King – though prudence well
Have taught thy subject to rebel –

And am I wrong, to worship where
Faith cannot doubt, nor Hope despair,
Since my own soul can grant my prayer?
Speak, God of visions, plead for me,
And tell why I have chosen thee!   **40**

Remembrance

Cold in the earth and the deep snow piled above thee!
Far, far removed, cold in the dreary grave:
Have I forgot, my only Love, to love thee,
Severed at last by Time's all-severing wave?

Now, when alone, do my thoughts no longer hover
Over the mountains on Angora's shore;
Resting their wings where heath and fern-leaves cover
That noble heart for ever, ever more?

Cold in the earth, and fifteen wild Decembers
From these brown hills have melted into spring –   **10**
Faithful indeed is the spirit that remembers
After such years of change and suffering!

Sweet Love of youth, forgive if I forget thee
While the World's tide is bearing me along:
Other desires and other Hopes beset me,
Hopes which obscure but cannot do thee wrong.

No later light has lightened up my heavens;
No second morn has ever shone for me;
All my life's bliss from thy dear life was given –
All my life's bliss is in the grave with thee.   **20**

But when the days of golden dreams had perished
And even Despair was powerless to destroy,
Then did I learn how existence could be cherished,
Strengthened and fed without the aid of joy.

Then did I check the tears of useless passion,
Weaned my young soul from yearning after thine;
Sternly denied its burning wish to hasten
Down to that tomb already more than mine!

And even yet, I dare not let it languish,
Dare not indulge in Memory's rapturous pain;   30
Once drinking deep of that divinest anguish,
How could I seek the empty world again?

'No coward soul is mine'

No coward soul is mine,
No trembler in the world's storm-troubled sphere;
I see Heaven's glories shine
And Faith shines equal arming me from Fear.

O God within my breast,
Almighty ever-present Deity
Life, that in me hast rest
As I, Undying Life, have power in Thee.

Vain are the thousand creeds
That move men's hearts, unutterably vain,   10
Worthless as withered weeds
Or idlest froth amid the boundless main

To waken doubt in one
Holding so fast by thy infinity,
So surely anchored on
The steadfast rock of Immortality.

With wide-embracing love
Thy spirit animates eternal years,
Pervades and broods above,
Changes, sustains, dissolves, creates and rears.   20

Though Earth and moon were gone
And suns and universes ceased to be
And thou wert left alone
Every Existence would exist in thee.

There is not room for Death
Nor atom that his might could render void
Since thou art Being and Breath
And what thou art may never be destroyed.

Stanzas*

Often rebuked, yet always back returning
   To those first feelings that were born with me,
And leaving busy chase of wealth and learning
   For idle dreams of things which cannot be:

Today, I will not seek the shadowy region;
   Its unsustaining vastness waxes drear;
And visions rising, legion after legion,
   Bring the unreal world too strangely near.

I'll walk, but not in old heroic traces,
   And not in paths of high morality,   10
And not among the half-distinguished faces
   The clouded forms of long-past history.

I'll walk where my own nature would be leading:
   It vexes me to choose another guide:
Where the grey flocks in ferny glens are feeding;
   Where the wild wind blows on the mountain side.

What have these lonely mountains worth revealing?
   More glory and more grief than I can tell:
The earth that wakes one human heart to feeling
   Can centre both the worlds of Heaven and Hell.   20

215

ANNE BRONTË
1820-1849

Song

We know where deepest lies the snow,
And where the frost-winds keenest blow,
   O'er every mountain's brow,
We long have known and learnt to bear
The wandering outlaw's toil and care,
But where we late were hunted, there
   Our foes are hunted now.

We have their princely homes, and they
To our wild haunts are chased away,
   Dark woods, and desert caves.   10
And we can range from hill to hill,
And chase our vanquished victors still;
Small respite will they find until
   They slumber in their graves.

But I would rather be the hare
That crouching in its sheltered lair
   Must start at every sound;
That forced from cornfields waving wide
Is driven to seek the bare hillside,
Or in the tangled copse to hide,   20
   Than be the hunter's hound.

JEAN INGELOW
1820-1897

Sing high! Though the red sun dip,
There yet is a day for me.

Born in Boston, Lincolnshire; father was a merchant trader; brought up in strict Evangelical faith; moved to Ipswich, 1834; first recorded writing verse on a window-shutter, when aged fourteen. *Poems, by Jean Ingelow* (1863) went through thirty editions. Went in for lengthy romantic yarns of love, heroism and disaster, in vigorous verse. Knew Jane Taylor, Dora Greenwell and Christina Rossetti; never married; lived a pious, retired life in London suburbs; her brother William's death was a great blow; buried in Brompton Cemetery.

Poetical Works (London: Longmans Green, 1902); Maureen Peters, *Jean Ingelow: Victorian Poetess* (Ipswich: Boydell, 1972).

from *Divided*

A dappled sky, a world of meadows,
　　Circling above us the black rooks fly
Forward, backward; lo their dark shadows
　　Flit on the blossoming tapestry.

Flit on the beck, for her long grass parteth
　　As hair from a maid's bright eyes blown back;
And lo, the sun like a lover darteth
　　His flattering smile on her wayward track.

Sing on! we sing in the glorious weather
　　Till one steps over the tiny strand,　　　　　　10
So narrow, in sooth, that still together
　　On either brink we go hand in hand.

The beck grows wider, the hands must sever.
　　On either margin, our songs all done,
We move apart, while she singeth ever,
　　Taking the course of the stooping sun.

He prays, 'Come over' – I may not follow;
I cry, 'Return' – but he cannot come:
We speak, we laugh, but with voices hollow;
   Our hands are hanging, our hearts are numb.   **20**

The High Tide on the Coast of Lincolnshire, 1571*

The old mayor climbed the belfry tower,
   The ringers ran by two, by three;
'Pull, if ye never pulled before;
   Good ringers, pull your best,' quoth he.
'Play up, play up, O Boston bells!
Ply all your changes, all your swells,
   Play up "The Brides of Enderby".'

Men say it was a stolen tide –
   The Lord that sent it, He knows all;
But in mine ears doth still abide   **10**
   The message that the bells let fall:
And there was nought of strange, beside
The flights of mews and peewits pied
   By millions crouched on the old sea wall.

I sat and spun within the door,
   My thread brake off, I raised mine eyes;
The level sun, like ruddy ore,
   Lay sinking in the barren skies,
And dark against day's golden death
She moved where Lindis wandereth,   **20**
   My son's fair wife, Elizabeth.

'Cusha! Cusha! Cusha!' calling,
Ere the early dews were falling,
Far away I heard her song.
'Cusha! Cusha!' all along
Where the reedy Lindis floweth,

218

Floweth, floweth;
From the meads where melic groweth
Faintly came her milking song –

'Cusha! Cusha! Cusha!' calling,   30
'For the dews will soon be falling;
Leave your meadow grasses mellow,
    Mellow, mellow;
Quit your cowslips, cowslips yellow;
Come up Whitefoot, come up Lightfoot,
Quit the stalks of parsley hollow,
    Hollow, hollow;
Come up Jetty, rise and follow,
From the clovers lift your head;
Come up Whitefoot, come up Lightfoot,   40
Come up Jetty, rise and follow,
Jetty, to the milking shed.'

If it be long, ay, long ago,
    When I begin to think how long,
Again I hear the Lindis flow,
    Swift as an arrow, sharp and strong;
And all the air, it seemeth me,
Is full of floating bells (saith she),
That ring the tune of Enderby.

All fresh the level pasture lay,   50
    And not a shadow might be seen,
Save where full five good miles away
    The steeple towered from out the green;
And lo! the great bell far and wide
Was heard in all the country side
That Saturday at eventide.

The swanherds where their sedges are
    Moved on in sunset's golden breath,
The shepherd lads I heard afar,

And my son's wife, Elizabeth;   60
Till floating o'er the grassy sea
Came down that kindly message free,
The 'Brides of Mavis Enderby'.

Then some looked up into the sky,
    And all along where Lindis flows
To where the goodly vessels lie,
    And where the lordly steeple shows.
They said, 'And why should this thing be?
What danger lowers by land or sea?
They ring the tune of Enderby!   70

'For evil news from Mablethorpe,
    Of pirate galleys warping down;
For ships ashore beyond the scorpe,
    They have not spared to wake the town;
But while the west is red to see,
And storms be none, and pirates flee,
Why ring "The Brides of Enderby"?'

I looked without, and lo! my son
    Came riding down with might and main:
He raised a shout as he drew on,   80
    Till all the welkin rang again,
'Elizabeth! Elizabeth!'
(A sweeter woman ne'er drew breath
Than my son's wife, Elizabeth.)

'The old sea wall (he cried) is down,
    The rising tide comes on apace,
And boats adrift in yonder town
    Go sailing up the market-place.'
He shook as one that looks on death:
'God save you, mother,' straight he saith;   90
'Where is my wife, Elizabeth?'

220

'Good son, where Lindis winds away,
    With her two bairns I marked her long;
And ere yon bells began to play
    Afar I heard her milking song.'
He looked across the grassy lea,
To right, to left, 'Ho Enderby!'
They rang 'The Brides of Enderby!'

With that he cried and beat his breast;
    For, lo! along the river's bed   100
A mighty eygre reared his crest,
    And up the Lindis raging sped.
It swept with thunderous noises loud;
Shaped like a curling snow-white cloud,
Or like a demon in a shroud.

And rearing Lindis backward pressed
    Shook all her trembling banks amain;
Then madly at the eygre's breast
    Flung up her weltering walls again.
Then banks came down with ruin and rout – 110
Then beaten foam flew round about –
Then all the mighty floods were out.

So far, so fast the eygre drave,
    The heart had hardly time to beat,
Before a shallow seething wave
    Sobbed in the grasses at our feet:
The feet had hardly time to flee
Before it brake against the knee,
And all the world was in the sea.

Upon the roof we sat that night,   120
    The noise of bells went sweeping by;
I marked the lofty beacon light
    Stream from the church, red and high –
A lurid mark and dread to see;

And awesomè bells they were to me,
That in the dark rang 'Enderby'.

They rang the sailor lads to guide
　　From roof to roof who fearless rowed;
And I – my son was at my side,
　　And yet the ruddy beacon glowed;　　　　130
And yet he moaned beneath his breath,
'O come in life, or come in death!
O lost! my love, Elizabeth.'

* * *

I shall never see her more
Where the reeds and rushes quiver,
　　Shiver, quiver;
Stand beside the sobbing river,
Sobbing, throbbing, in its falling
To the sandy lonesome shore;
I shall never hear her calling,　　　　140
Leave your meadow grasses mellow,
　　Mellow, mellow;
Quit your cowslips, cowslips yellow;
Come up Whitefoot, come up Lightfoot;
Quit your pipes of parsley hollow,
　　Hollow, hollow;
Come up Lightfoot, rise and follow;
　　Lightfoot, Whitefoot,
From your clovers lift the head;
Come up Jetty, follow, follow,
Jetty, to the milking shed.

DORA GREENWELL
1821-1882

Only daughter of five children of Dorothy (Smales) and William Green-
well, a squire of County Durham. First volume, *Poems*, 1848; others in
1861 and 1867; religious verse, *Carmina Crucis*, 1869. Had strong Evangel-
ical sympathies, wrote on religious matters and social problems (child
labour, the cotton famine, for example). Lived mostly in the north, with
her parents, and later with her brother.

Constance L. Maynard (ed. and intro.), *Selected Poems of Dora Greenwell*
(London, 1906); H. Bett, *Dora Greenwell* (London: Epworth, 1950).

A Scherzo
A Shy Person's Wishes

With the wasp at the innermost heart of a peach,
On a sunny wall out of tip-toe reach,
With the trout in the darkest summer pool,
With the fern-seed clinging behind its cool
Smooth frond, in the chink of an aged tree,
In the woodbine's horn with the drunken bee,
With the mouse in its nest in a furrow old,
With the chrysalis wrapped in its gauzy fold;
With things that are hidden, and safe, and bold,
With things that are timid, and shy, and free,   10
Wishing to be;
With the nut in its shell, with the seed in its pod,
With the corn as it sprouts in the kindly clod,
Far down where the secret of beauty shows
In the bulb of the tulip, before it blows;
With things that are rooted, and firm, and deep,
Quiet to lie, and dreamless to sleep;
With things that are chainless, and tameless, and proud,
With the fire in the jagged thunder-cloud,
With the wind in its sleep, with the wind in its waking,   20
With the drops that go to the rainbow's making,

Wishing to be with the light leaves shaking,
Or stones in some desolate highway breaking;
Far up on the hills, where no foot surprises
The dew as it falls, or the dust as it rises;
To be couched with the beast in its torrid lair,
Or drifting on ice with the polar bear,
With the weaver at work at his quiet loom;
Anywhere, anywhere, out of this room!

The Sunflower

Till the slow daylight pale,
　　A willing slave, fast bound to one above,
I wait; he seems to speed, and change, and fail;
　　I know he will not move.

I lift my golden orb
　　To his, unsmitten when the roses die,
And in my broad and burning disk absorb
　　The splendours of his eye.

His eye is like a clear
　　Keen flame that searches through me: I must droop　　10
Upon my stalk, I cannot reach his sphere;
　　To mine he cannot stoop.

I win not my desire,
　　And yet I fail not of my guerdon; lo!
A thousand flickering darts and tongues of fire
　　Around me spread and glow.

All rayed and crowned, I miss
　　No queenly state until the summer wane,
The hours flit by; none knoweth of my bliss,
　　And none has guessed my pain.　　20

I follow one above,
   I track the shadow of his steps, I grow
Most like to him I love
   Of all that shines below.

CHRISTINA ROSSETTI
1830-1893

The fourth child of an English mother, Frances (Polidori), and Gabriele Rossetti, an Italian political exile, later Professor of Italian at London University; he lapsed from Catholicism, but his wife and daughters became devout Anglo-Catholics. Educated at home; first *Waves* published 1847; incorrect diagnosis of tuberculosis. An early romance with James Collinson, a member of her brother Dante Gabriel Rossetti's Pre-Raphaelite Brotherhood; in 1847 met William Bell Scott, suggested as the secret 'love of her life'. Undertook charitable work at Home for Fallen Women, 1860-70. *Goblin Market* volume (1862), praised by Gosse as 'brilliant, fantastic, and profoundly original' (unfortunately, her great poem is far too long for inclusion here); in that year met another wooer, the scholar Charles Bagot Cayley. In 1866 gave up hopes of Scott, but rejected Cayley, possibly on religious grounds. In 1870 diagnosed as suffering from thyroidic illness, that left her with a swollen throat, brown skin, hair loss and headaches, though she partially recovered. *Collected Poems* published 1875. Her later years seem to have been retired, devout and not happy. For all her insistent melancholy, self-repression, self-deferral and religious anxiety, her poetry has a passion and intensity matched by few in that century: denial was what she felt, and sought; deprivation produced an obstinate identity.

W.M. Rossetti (ed.), *The Poetical Works of Christina Georgina Rossetti* (London: Macmillan, 1904); Kathleen Blake, *Love and the Woman Question in Victorian Literature* (Brighton: Harvester; New Jersey: Barnes and Noble, 1983); A.H. Harrison, *Christina Rossetti in Context* (Brighton: Harvester, 1989).

Remember

Remember me when I am gone away,
  Gone far away into the silent land;
  When you can no more hold me by the hand,
Nor I half turn to go yet turning stay.
Remember me when no more day by day
  You tell me of our future that you planned:

Only remember me; you understand
It will be late then to counsel or to pray.
Yet if you should forget me for a while
    And afterwards remember, do not grieve: 10
    For if the darkness and corruption leave
    A vestige of the thoughts that once I had,
Better by far you should forget and smile
    Than that you should remember and be sad.

The World

By day she woos me, soft, exceeding fair:
    But all night as the moon so changeth she;
    Loathsome and foul as hidden leprosy
And subtle serpents gliding in her hair.
By day she woos me to the outer air,
    Ripe fruits, sweet flowers, and full satiety:
    But through the night, a beast she grins at me,
A very monster void of love and prayer.
By day she stands a lie: by night she stands
    In all the naked horror of the truth,   10
With pushing horns and clawed and clutching hands.
Is this a friend indeed, that I should sell
    My soul to her, give her my life and youth,
Till my feet, cloven too, take hold on hell?

From the Antique

It's a weary life, it is, she said: –
    Doubly blank in a woman's lot:
I wish and wish I were a man:
    Or, better than any being, were not:

Were nothing at all in all the world,
    Not a body and not a soul:

Not so much as a grain of dust
   Or drop of water from pole to pole.

Still the world would wag on the same,
   Still the seasons go and come: 10
Blossoms bloom as in days of old,
   Cherries ripen and wild bees hum.

None would miss me in all the world,
   How much less would care or weep:
I should be nothing, while all the rest
   Would wake and weary and fall asleep.

Echo

Come to me in the silence of the night;
   Come in the speaking silence of a dream;
Come with soft rounded cheeks and eyes as bright
   As sunlight on a stream;
     Come back in tears,
O memory, hope, love of finished years.

O dream how sweet, too sweet, too bitter sweet,
   Whose wakening should have been in Paradise,
Where souls brimfull of love abide and meet;
   Where thirsting longing eyes   10
     Watch the slow door
That opening, letting in, lets out no more.

Yet come to me in dreams, that I may live
   My very life again though cold in death:
Come back to me in dreams, that I may give
   Pulse for pulse, breath for breath:
     Speak low, lean low,
As long ago, my love, how long ago.

In An Artist's Studio*

One face looks out from all his canvases,
     One selfsame figure sits or walks or leans:
     We found her hidden just behind those screens,
That mirror gave back all her loveliness.
A queen in opal or in ruby dress,
     A nameless girl in freshest summer-greens,
     A saint, an angel – every canvas means
The same one meaning, neither more nor less.
He feeds upon her face by day and night,
     And she with true kind eyes looks back on him,   10
Fair as the moon and joyful as the light:
     Not wan with waiting, nor with sorrow dim;
Not as she is, but was when hope shone bright;
     Not as she is, but as she fills his dream.

A Birthday

My heart is like a singing bird
     Whose nest is in a watered shoot;
My heart is like an apple-tree
     Whose boughs are bent with thickest fruit;
My heart is like a rainbow shell
     That paddles in a halcyon sea;
My heart is gladder than all these
     Because my love is come to me.

Raise me a dais of silk and down;
     Hang it with vair and purple dyes;   10
Carve it in doves, and pomegranates,
     And peacocks with a hundred eyes;
Work it in gold and silver grapes,
     In leaves, and silver fleurs-de-lys;
Because the birthday of my life
     Is come, my love is come to me.

229

Up-Hill

Does the road wind up-hill all the way?
    Yes, to the very end.
Will the day's journey take the whole long day?
    From morn to night, my friend.

But is there for the night a resting-place?
    A roof for when the slow dark hours begin.
May not the darkness hide it from my face?
    You cannot miss that inn.

Shall I meet other wayfarers at night?
    Those who have gone before.   10
Then must I knock, or call when just in sight?
    They will not keep you standing at that door.

Shall I find comfort, travel-sore and weak?
    Of labour you shall find the sum.
Will there be beds for me and all who seek?
    Yea, beds for all who come.

Amor Mundi

'Oh where are you going with your love-locks flowing,
    On the west wind blowing along this valley track?'
'The downhill path is easy, come with me an it please ye,
    We shall escape the uphill by never turning back.'

So they two went together in glowing August weather,
    The honey-breathing heather lay to their left and right;
And dear she was to dote on, her swift feet seemed to float on
    The air like soft twin pigeons too sportive to alight.

'Oh, what is that in heaven where grey cloud-flakes are seven,
    Where blackest clouds hang riven just at the rainy skirt?'   10

'Oh, that's a meteor sent us, the message dumb, portentous, –
    An undeciphered solemn signal of help or hurt.'

'Oh, what is that glides quickly where velvet flowers grow thickly,
    Their scent comes rich and sickly?' – 'A scaled and hooded worm.'
'Oh, what's that in the hollow, so pale I quake to follow?'
    'Oh, that's a thin dead body which waits the eternal term.'

'Turn again, O my sweetest, – turn again, false and fleetest:
    This way whereof thou weetest I fear is hell's own track.'
'Nay, too steep for hill-mounting; nay, too late for cost counting:
    This downhill path is easy, but there's no turning back.'   20

The Thread of Life

I

The irresponsive silence of the land,
    The irresponsive sounding of the sea,
    Speak both one message of one sense to me: –
'Aloof, aloof, we stand aloof, so stand
Thou too aloof bound with the flawless band
    Of inner solitude; we bind not thee;
    But who from thy self-chain shall set thee free?
What heart shall touch thy heart? What hand thy hand?'
And I am sometimes proud and sometimes meek,
    And sometimes I remember days of old   10
When fellowship seemed not so far to seek
    And all the world and I seemed much less cold,
    And at the rainbow's foot lay surely gold,
And hope felt strong and life itself not weak.

II

Thus am I mine own prison. Everything
    Around me free and sunny and at ease:
    Or if in shadow, in a shade of trees
Which the sun kisses, where the gay birds sing

231

And where all winds make various murmuring;
  Where bees are found, with honey for the bees;
  Where sounds are music, and where silences
Are music of an unlike fashioning.
Then gaze I at the merrymaking crew
  And smile a moment and a moment sigh   10
Thinking: Why can I not rejoice with you?
  But soon I put the foolish fancy by:
I am not what I have nor what I do;
  But what I was I am, I am even I.

III

Therefore myself is that one only thing
  I hold to use or waste, to keep or give;
  My sole possession every day I live,
And still mine own despite Time's winnowing.
Ever mine own, while moon and seasons bring
  From crudeness ripeness mellow and sanative;
  Ever mine own, when saints break grave and sing.
And this myself as king unto my King
  I give, to Him who gave Himself for me;   10
Who gives Himself to me, and bids me sing
  A sweet new song of His redeemed set free;
He bids me sing, O Death, where is thy sting?
  And sing, O grave, where is thy victory?

LOUISA S. BEVINGTON
later GUGGENBERGER
b.1845

The eldest of eight children of Alexander Bevington, a Quaker, who encouraged her interest in nature and writing. Embarked on a literary career, writing articles and poems on evolutionism, read by Darwin. In 1883 married a Munich artist, Ignatz Guggenberger, and lived in Meran and then in London; in her later years became an enthusiastic anarchist-communist. Her espousal of energy, lively response to the natural world, strong sense of social indignation and of passion, provide a refreshing note in late Victorian poetry.

Key-Notes (London, 1876, 1879); *Poems, Lyrics and Sonnets* (London, 1882); *Liberty Lyrics* (London, 1895), produced by *Liberty: A Journal of Anarchist Communism*, ed. James Tochalti, whose contributors included Kropotkin, Shaw and William Morris.

Morning

What's the text today for reading
Nature and its being by?
There is effort all the morning
Thro' the windy sea and sky.

All, intent in earnest grapple
That the All may let it be:
Force, in unity, at variance
With its own diversity.

Force, prevailing unto action,
Force, persistent to restrain,   10
In a twofold, one-souled wrestle
Forging Being's freedom-chain.

Frolic! say you – when the billow
Tosses back a mane of spray?
No; but haste of earnest effort;
Nature works in guise of play.

Till the balance shall be even
Swings the to and fro of strife;
Till an awful equilibrium
Stills it, beats the Heart of Life.   20

What's the text today for reading
Nature and its being by?
Effort, effort all the morning,
Thro' the windy sea and sky.

Afternoon

Purple headland over yonder,
    Fleecy, sun-extinguished moon,
I am here alone, and ponder
    On the theme of Afternoon.

Past has made a groove for Present,
    And what fits it *is*: no more.
Waves before the wind are weighty;
    Strongest sea-beats shape the shore.

Just what is is just what can be,
    And the Possible is free;   10
'Tis by being, not by effort,
    That the firm cliff juts to sea.

With an uncontentious calmness
    Drifts the Fact before the 'Law';
So we name the ordered sequence
    We, remembering, foresaw.

234

And a law is mere procession
    Of the forcible and fit;
Calm of uncontested Being,
    And our thought that comes of it.   20

In the mellow shining daylight
    Lies the Afternoon at ease,
Little willing ripples answer
    To a drift of casual breeze.

Purple headland to the westward!
    Ebbing tide, and fleecy moon!
In the 'line of least resistance',
    Flows the life of Afternoon.

Twilight

Grey the sky, and growing dimmer,
    And the twilight lulls the sea;
Half in vagueness, half in glimmer,
    Nature shrouds her mystery.

What have all the hours been spent for?
    Why the on and on of things?
Why eternity's procession
    Of the days and evenings?

Hours of sunshine, hours of gloaming,
    Wing their unexplaining flight,   10
With a measured punctuation
    Of unconsciousness, at night.

Just at sunset was translucence,
    When the west was all aflame;
So I asked the sea a question,
    And an answer nearly came.

Is there nothing but Occurrence?
    Though each detail seem an Act,
Is that whole we deem so pregnant
    But unemphasized Fact?   20

Or, when dusk is in the hollows
    Of the hill-side and the wave,
Are things so much in earnest
    That they cannot but be grave?

Nay, the lesson of the Twilight
    Is as simple as 'tis deep;
Acquiescence, acquiescence,
    And the coming on of sleep.

Midnight

There are sea and sky about me,
    And yet nothing sense can mark;
For a mist fills all the midnight
    Adding blindness to the dark.

There is not the faintest echo
    From the life of yesterday:
Not the vaguest stir foretelling
    Of a morrow on the way.

'Tis negation's hour of triumph
    In the absence of the sun;   10
'Tis the hour of endings, ended,
    Of beginnings, unbegun.

Yet the voice of awful silence
    Bids my waiting spirit hark;
There is action in the stillness,
    There is progress in the dark.

236

In the drift of things and forces
   Comes the better from the worse;
Swings the whole of Nature upward,
   Wakes, and thinks – a universe.   20

There will be *more* life tomorrow,
   And *of* life, more life that *knows*;
Though the sum of force be constant
   Yet the Living ever grows.

So we sing of evolution,
   And step strongly on our ways;
And we live through nights in patience,
   And we learn the worth of days.

from *Two songs*
WITH THE TIDE: A CRY OF WEAKNESS

Deep, and silent, and wide,
   The evening shelters are spread;
   And the tears may flow unread
   That the taunt of day would have dried.
And oh! most dear love of mine, we may float one hour with the tide.

I see the great river go,
   Fast, where the lamplight gleams
   In streaks: – I see how it streams
   Through a moment's revealing glow;
Like a life, from the dark to the dark, that flows because it must flow.

And the old church-bells divide
   The moments of evening-time;
   As a passion-charged soul they chime,
   As a sob of near bliss outside,
And the wild vague flow goes on of the tacit, unhindering tide.

My love! my love! are you there
  In this hour of stealing drift?
  When through every quivering rift
  Of silence there strays an air
Like a whisper of blessed sanction, answering a hopeless prayer.

I see with a dreamy sight, –
  I hear with a half-lent ear, –
  How the bells keep showering near,
  How the wild flood hurries tonight;
And lamps on the farther shore keep lending long gleams of light.

O reckless of source or end,
  Let the great river go!
  Adrift on its bosom's flow
  One infinite hour to spend;
Hark! how the sobbing bells from silence to silence tend.

There is all day long for the fight
  With the deep perverseness of life;
  We may rest one hour from the strife,
  As the heavens may rest from light.
O love! with your lips on mine, drift, drift with the tide, tonight.

Wrestling

Our oneness is the wrestlers', fierce and close,
    Thrusting and thrust;
One life in dual effort for one prize, –
    We fight, and must;
For soul with soul does battle evermore
    Till love be trust.

Our distance is love's severance; sense divides,
    Each is but each;
Never the very hidden spirit of thee

My life doth reach;
Twain! since love athwart the gulf that needs
    Kisses and speech.

Ah! wrestle closelier! we draw nearer so
    Than any bliss
Can bring twain souls who would be whole and one,
    Too near to kiss:
To be one thought, one voice before we die, –
    Wrestle for this.

ALICE MEYNELL
1847-1922

Her father, Thomas James Thompson, a writer, and her mother, Christiana (Weller), a talented pianist, were friends of Dickens. While still a girl, entered the Roman Catholic church. Her first volume, *Preludes*, published 1875, was praised by Ruskin and Dante Gabriel Rossetti. She wrote, 'Whatever I write will be melancholy and self-conscious, as are all women's poems', and complained of 'the miserable selfishness of men that keeps women from work'. In 1876 married Wilfred Meynell, a Catholic journalist, and began a hectic life, bringing up seven children while co-editing several magazines, and writing twelve volumes of essays and eight of poetry. Her verse was carefully worked, written, 'one might believe, with an etching pen', commented Vita Sackville-West, who also reported that 'she took particular pains in the use of draped garments and high heels to make herself appear as tall as possible'; she expressed liberal political views, was a vigorous feminist and, later, a suffragist and pacifist (her sister, Lady Elizabeth Butler, was a distinguished painter of military life and action).

Frederick Page (ed.), *Poems of Alice Meynell* (Oxford: OUP, 1940); June Badeni, *The Slender Tree: A Life of Alice Meynell* (Padstow, 1981).

Renouncement

I must not think of thee; and, tired yet strong,
   I shun the thought that lurks in all delight –
   The thought of thee – and in the blue Heaven's height,
And in the sweetest passage of a song.

Oh, just beyond the fairest thoughts that throng
   This breast, the thought of thee waits, hidden though bright;
   Yet it must never, never come in sight;
I must stop short of thee the whole day long.

But when sleep comes to close each difficult day,
   When night gives pause to the long watch I keep,   10
     And all my bonds I needs must loose apart,

Must doff my will as raiment laid away, –
  With the first dream that comes with the first sleep
  I run, I run, I am gathered to thy heart.

The Shepherdess

She walks – the lady of my delight –
  A shepherdess of sheep.
Her flocks are thoughts. She keeps them white;
  She guards them from the steep;
She feeds them on the fragrant height,
  And folds them in for sleep.

She roams maternal hills and bright,
  Dark valleys safe and deep.
Into that tender breast at night
  The chastest stars may peep.   10
She walks – the lady of my delight –
  A shepherdess of sheep.

She holds her little thoughts in sight,
  Though gay they run and leap.
She is so circumspect and right;
  She has her soul to keep.
She walks – the lady of my delight –
  The shepherdess of sheep.

Maternity

One wept whose only child was dead,
  New-born, ten years ago.
'Weep not; he is in bliss,' they said.
  She answered, 'Even so.
Ten years ago was born in pain
  A child, not now forlorn.

But oh, ten years ago, in vain
A mother, a mother was born.'

Parentage

'When Augustus Caesar legislated against the unmarried citizens of
Rome, he declared them to be, in some sort, slayers of the people.'

Ah no! not these!
These, who were childless, are not they who gave
So many dead unto the journeying wave,
The helpless nurslings of the cradling seas;
Not they who doomed by infallible decrees
Unnumbered man to the innumerable grave.

But those who slay
Are fathers. Theirs are armies. Death is theirs –
The death of innocences and despairs;
The dying of the golden and the grey.   10
The sentence, when they speak it, has no Nay.
And she who slays is she who bears, who bears.

A Dead Harvest
In Kensington Gardens

Along the graceless grass of town
They rake the rows of red and brown, –
Dead leaves, unlike the rows of hay
Delicate, touched with gold and grey,
Raked long ago and far away.

A narrow silence in the park,
Between the lights a narrow dark.
One street rolls on the north; and one,
Muffled, upon the south doth run;
Amid the mist the work is done.   10

A futile crop! – for it the fire
Smoulders, and, for a stack, a pyre.
So go the town's lives on the breeze,
Even as the shedding of the trees;
Bosom nor barn is filled with these.

Chimes

Brief, in a flying night,
   From the shaken tower,
A flock of bells take flight,
   And go with the hour.

Like birds from the cote to the gales,
   Abrupt – O hark!
A fleet of bells set sails,
   And go to the dark.

Sudden the cold airs swing.
   Alone, aloud,   10
A verse of bells takes wing
   And flies with the cloud.

EDITH NESBIT
1858-1924

Fourth surviving child of Sarah (Alderton) and John Nesbit, head of an agricultural college in Kennington, who died when she was four. In 1880 married Hubert Bland, a small businessman (first child born two months later), who was both unfaithful and unsuccessful, so that she had to turn to writing – very successfully. Produced much children's fiction, notably *The Story of the Treasure Seekers* (1899), *The Wouldbegoods* (1901), and *The Railway Children* (1906). Socialist, a member of the Fabian society, loved George Bernard Shaw, unavailingly (as usual). Bland died in 1914, and in 1917 she married Thomas Tucker, a retired marine engineer.

Lays and Legends (London, 1886); *Leaves of Life* (London, 1888); *A Pomander of Verse* (London, 1895); Julia Briggs, *A Woman of Passion: The Life of Edith Nesbit* (London: Hutchinson, 1987).

Song

Oh, baby, baby, baby dear,
We lie alone together here;
The snowy gown and cap and sheet
With lavender are fresh and sweet;
Through half-closed blinds the roses peer
To see and love you, baby dear.

We are so tired, we like to lie
Just doing nothing, you and I
Within the darkened quiet room.
The sun sends dusk rays through the gloom,   10
Which is no gloom since you are here,
My little life, my baby dear.

Soft sleepy mouth so vaguely pressed
Against your new-made mother's breast,
Soft little hands in mine I fold,

Soft little feet I kiss and hold,
Round soft smooth head and tiny ear,
All mine, my own, my baby dear.

And he we love is far away!
But he will come some happy day,   20
You need but me, and I can rest
At peace with you beside me pressed.
There are no questions, longings vain,
No murmurings, nor doubt, nor pain,
Only content and we are here,
        My baby dear.

Among His Books*

A silent room – grey with a dusty blight
        Of loneliness;
A room with not enough of light
        Its form to dress.

Books enough though! The groaning sofa bears
        A goodly store –
Books on the window-seat, and on the chairs,
        And on the floor.

Books of all sorts of soul, all sorts of age,
        All sorts of face –   10
Black-letter, vellum, and the flimsy page
        Of commonplace.

All bindings, from the cloth whose hue distracts
        One's weary nerves,
To yellow parchment, binding rare old tracts
        It serves – deserves.

Books on the shelves, and in the cupboard books,
    Worthless and rare –
Books on the mantelpiece – wheree'er one looks
    Books everywhere!   20

Books! books! the only things in life I find
    Not wholly vain.
Books in my hands – books in my heart enshrined –
    Books in my brain.

My friends are they: for children and for wife
    They serve me too;
For these alone, of all dear things in life,
    Have I found true.

They do not flatter, change, deny, deceive –
    Ah no – not they!   30
The same editions which one night you leave
    You find next day.

You don't find railway novels where you left
    Your Elzevirs!
Your Aldines don't betray you – leave bereft
    Your lonely years!

And yet this common book of Common Prayer
    My heart prefers,
Because the names upon the fly-leaf there
    Are mine and hers.   40

It's a dead flower that makes it open so –
    Forget-me-not –
The Marriage Service . . . well, my dear, you know
    Who first forgot.

Those were the days when in the choir we two
    Sat – used to sing –
When I believed in God, in love, in you –
    In everything.

Through quiet lanes to church we used to come,
    Happy and good,   50
Clasp hands through sermon, and go slowly home
    Down through the wood.

Kisses? A certain yellow rose no doubt
    That porch still shows,
Whenever I hear kisses talked about
    I smell that rose!

No – I don't blame you – since you only proved
    My choice unwise,
And taught me books should trusted be and loved,
    Not lips and eyes!   60

And so I keep your book – your flower – to show
    How much I care
For the dear memory of what, you know,
    You never were.

The Gray Folk

The house, with blind unhappy face,
    Stands lonely in the last year's corn,
    And in the grayness of the morn
The gray folk come about the place.

By many pathways, gliding gray
    They come past meadow, wood, and wold,
    Come by the farm and by the fold
From the green fields of yesterday.

247

Past lock and chain and bolt and bar
   They press, to stand about my bed,   **10**
   And like the faces of the dead
I know their hidden faces are.

They will not leave me in the day
   And when night falls they will not go,
   Because I silenced, long ago,
The only voice they will obey.

Villeggiature

My window, framed in pear-tree bloom,
   White-curtained shone, and softly lighted:
So, by the pear-tree to my room
   Your ghost last night climbed uninvited.

Your solid self, long leagues away,
   Deep in dull books, had hardly missed me;
And yet you found this Romeo's way,
   And through the blossom climbed and kissed me.

I watched the still and dewy lawn,
   The pear-tree boughs hung white above you;   **10**
I listened to you till the dawn,
   And half forgot I did not love you.

Oh, dear! what pretty things you said,
   What pearls of song you threaded for me!
I did not – till your ghost had fled –
   Remember how you always bore me!

AMY LEVY
1861-1889

Parents Isabelle (Levin) and Lewis Levy; first Jewish woman to enter Newnham College, Cambridge, where published first volume of verse. Friend of Oscar Wilde, Olive Schreiner and Richard Garnett; travelled on the Continent, writing on Jewish affairs; novel, *Reuben Sachs*, published 1888; melancholic, feminist, radical, she committed suicide.

Xantippe and Other Verse (London, 1881); *A Minor Poet and Other Verse* (London, 1884); *A London Plane Tree and Other Verse* (London, 1889).

London Poets

They trod the streets and squares where now I tread,
With weary hearts, a little while ago;
When, thin and grey, the melancholy snow
Clung to the leafless branches overhead;
Or when the smoke-veiled sky grew stormy-red
In autumn; with a re-arisen woe
Wrestled, what time the passionate spring winds blow.

And paced scorched stones in summer: – they are dead.
The sorrow of their souls to them did seem
As real as mine to me, as permanent.   10
Today, it is the shadow of a dream,
The half-forgotten breath of breezes spent.
So shall another soothe his woe supreme –
'No more he comes, who this way came and went.'

Epitaph
(On a commonplace person who died in bed)

This is the end of him, here he lies:
The dust in his throat, the worm in his eyes,
The mould in his mouth, the turf on his breast;

This is the end of him, this is best.
He will never lie on his couch awake,
Wide-eyed, tearless, till dim daybreak.
Never again will he smile and smile
When his heart is breaking all the while.
He will never stretch out his hands in vain
Groping and groping – never again.   10
Never ask for bread, get a stone instead,
Never pretend that the stone is bread.
Never sway and sway 'twixt the false and true,
Weighing and noting the long hours through.
Never ache and ache with the chok'd-up sighs;
This is the end of him, here he lies.

A London Plane-Tree

Green is the plane-tree in the square,
    The other trees are brown;
They droop and pine for country air;
    The plane-tree loves the town.

Here from my garret-pane, I mark
    The plane-tree bud and blow,
Shed her recuperative bark,
    And spread her shade below.

Among her branches, in and out,
    The city breezes play;   10
The dim fog wraps her round about;
    Above, the smoke curls grey.

Others the country take for choice,
    And hold the town in scorn;
But she has listened to the voice
    On city breezes borne.

In the Mile End Road

How like her! But 'tis she herself,
  Comes up the crowded street,
How little did I think, the morn,
  My only love to meet?

Whose else that motion and that mien?
  Whose else that airy tread?
For one strange moment I forgot
  My only love was dead.

The Old House

In through the porch and up the silent stair;
  Little is changed, I know so well the ways; –
Here, the dead came to meet me; it was there
  The dream was dreamed in unforgotten days.

But who is this that hurries on before,
  A flitting shade the brooding shades among? –
She turned, – I saw her face, – O God, it wore
  The face I used to wear when I was young!

I thought my spirit and my heart were tamed
  To deadness; dead the pains that agonise.   10
The old griefs spring to choke me, – I am shamed
  Before that little ghost with eager eyes.

O turn away, let her not see, not know!
  How should she bear it, how should understand?
O hasten down the stairway, haste and go,
  And leave her dreaming in the silent land.

MARY COLERIDGE
1861-1907

'Poetry,' she wrote, 'is, by its very derivation, *making*, not feeling. But the odd thing is, I think, that what is most carefully made often sounds as if it had been felt straight off, whereas what has been felt carelessly sounds as if it were made.' Her father, Arthur Coleridge, great-nephew of S.T. Coleridge, was a lawyer and skilful amateur musician; her mother, Mary Ann Jameson. Privately highly educated; lived with her parents, travelled on the Continent, published essays and five novels. Friends spoke of her sensitivity and animation, a mind 'as sudden as the flight of a moth by candlelight'. Robert Bridges encouraged her to publish two volumes, but the rest of her verse was published posthumously by Sir Henry Newbolt, husband of her friend Margaret Duckworth. During the last twelve years of her life taught at the Working Women's College in London.

Theresa Whistler (ed. and intro.), *The Collected Poems of Mary Coleridge* (London: Rupert Hart-Davis, 1954); *Gathered Leaves from the Prose of Mary E. Coleridge, With a Memoir by Edith Sichel* (London: Constable, 1910).

The Other Side of a Mirror

I sat before my glass one day,
   And conjured up a vision bare,
Unlike the aspects glad and gay,
   That erst were found reflected there –
The vision of a woman, wild
   With more than womanly despair.

Her hair stood back on either side
   A face bereft of loveliness.
It had no envy now to hide
   What once no man on earth could guess.   10
It formed the thorny aureole
   Of hard unsanctified distress.

Her lips were open – not a sound
    Came through the parted lines of red.
Whate'er it was, the hideous wound
    In silence and in secret bled.
No sigh relieved her speechless woe,
    She had no voice to speak her dread.

And in her lurid eyes there shone
    The dying flames of life's desire   20
Made mad because its hope was gone,
    And kindled at the leaping fire
Of jealousy, and fierce revenge,
    And strength that could not change nor tire.

Shade of a shadow in the glass,
    O set the crystal surface free!
Pass – as the fairer visions pass –
    Nor ever more return, to be
The ghost of a distracted hour,
    That heard me whisper, 'I am she!'   30

A Moment

The clouds had made a crimson crown
Above the mountains high.
The stormy sun was going down
In a stormy sky.

Why did you let your eyes so rest on me,
And hold your breath between?
In all the ages this can never be
As if it had not been.

253

In Dispraise of the Moon

I would not be the Moon, the sickly thing,
To summon owls and bats upon the wing;
For when the noble Sun is gone away,
She turns his night into a pallid day.

She hath no air, no radiance of her own,
That world unmusical of earth and stone.
She wakes her dim, uncoloured, voiceless hosts,
Ghost of the Sun, herself the sun of ghosts.

The mortal eyes that gaze too long on her
Of Reason's piercing ray defrauded are.   10
Light in itself doth feed the living brain;
That light, reflected, but makes darkness plain.

The Poison Flower

The poison flower that in my garden grew
Killed all the other flowers beside.
They withered off and died,
Because their fiery foe sucked up the dew.

When the sun shone, the poison flower breathed cold
And spread a chilly mist of dull disgrace.
They could not see his face,
Roses and lilies languished and grew old.

Wherefore I tore that flower up by the root,
And flung it on the rubbish heap to fade   10
Amid the havoc that itself had made.
I did not leave one shoot.

Fair is my garden as it once was fair.
Lilies and roses reign.
They drink the dew, they see the sun again;
But I rejoice no longer, walking there.

An Insincere Wish Addressed to a Beggar

We are not near enough to love,
    I can but pity all your woe;
For wealth has lifted me above,
    And falsehood set you down below.

If you were true, we still might be
    Brothers in something more than name;
And were I poor, your love to me
    Would make our differing bonds the same.

But golden gates between us stretch,
    Truth opens her forbidding eyes;   10
You can't forget that I am rich,
    Nor I that you are telling lies.

Love never comes but at love's call,
    And pity asks for him in vain;
Because I cannot give you all,
    You give me nothing back again.

And you are right with all your wrong,
    For less than all is nothing too;
May Heaven beggar me ere long,
    And Truth reveal herself to you!   20

Marriage

No more alone sleeping, no more alone waking,
  Thy dreams divided, thy prayers in twain;
Thy merry sisters tonight forsaking,
  Never shall we see, maiden, again.

Never shall we see thee, thine eyes glancing,
  Flashing with laughter and wild in glee,
Under the mistletoe kissing and dancing,
  Wantonly free.

There shall come a matron walking sedately,
  Low-voiced, gentle, wise in reply.   10
Tell me, O tell me, can I love her greatly?
  All for her sake must the maiden die!

The White Women
('From a legend of Malay, told by Hugh Clifford')

Where dwell the lovely, wild white women folk,
    Mortal to man?
They never bowed their necks beneath the yoke,
They dwelt alone when the first morning broke
    And Time began.

Taller are they than man, and very fair,
    Their cheeks are pale,
At sight of them the tiger in his lair,
The falcon hanging in the azure air,
    The eagles quail.   10

The deadly shafts their nervous hands let fly
    Are stronger than our strongest – in their form
Larger, more beauteous, carved amazingly,
And when they fight, the wild white women cry
    The war-cry of the storm.

Their words are not as ours. If man might go
      Among the waves of Ocean when they break
And hear them – hear the language of the snow
Falling on torrents – he might also know
      The tongue they speak.   20

Pure are they as the light; they never sinned,
      But when the rays of the eternal fire
Kindle the West, their tresses they unbind
And fling their girdles to the Western wind,
      Swept by desire.

Lo, maidens to the maidens then are born,
      Strong children of the maidens and the breeze,
Dreams are not – in the glory of the morn,
Seen through the gates of ivory and horn –
      More fair than these.   30

And none may find their dwelling. In the shade
      Primeval of the forest oaks they hide.
One of our race, lost in an awful glade,
Saw with his human eyes a wild white maid,
      And gazing, died.

Notes

Written with a Diamond
Queen Elizabeth was confined in Woodstock Palace 1554-5
1 *by* meaning of

The Doubt of Future Foes
11 *daughter of debate* Mary Queen of Scots

On Monsieur's Departure
Probably referring to the visit of the Duc d'Alençon (1582),
a disappointed suitor

Wyll and Testament
42 Sumptuary laws required people to dress according to status
45 *Cheap* Cheapside, near St Paul's   **51** *purl* thread twisted with
gold or silver   **53** *bongraces* cloth shades for protection from the
sun   **64** *gardes* ornamental borders   **65, 66** *artillery, dagges*
guns   **71** *handsome men . . . wed* apprentices   **88** *sessions*
Justice of the Peace's court   **94** *. . . got the sum* prisoners had to
pay discharge fees   **111** *Smithfield* site of a weekly market, and
of St Bartholomew's Fair   **116** *neat* oxen   **117** *Spital* hospital
of St Bartholomew, near Smithfield   **119** *Bedlam* St Mary of
Bethlehem's asylum for the insane   **123** *Bridewell* workhouse
128 *Inns of Court* lawyers' colleges   **159** *standish* inkstand

Psalm 58: Si Vere Utique
13 *aspic* the poisonous asp

Psalm 139: Domine, Probasti
6 *closet* a small study-room   **55** *brave* handsome

The Description of Cooke-ham
The Manor of Cookham, near Maidenhead   **2** *that Grace* Her
Grace, Margaret, Countess of Cumberland   **31** *Philomela* the
nightingale   **64** *defended Phoebus* protected against the sun
93 *sweet Lady* Anne Clifford, Countess of Dorset and friend of
Lady Mary Wroth   **112** *conster* construe, analyse

Sonnets from Pamphilia to Amphilanthus: 68
5 *Goodwins* Goodwin Sands, off the Kentish coast

The Prologue
8 *Great Bartas* Guillaume Du Bartas, author of an epic poem on Christian history   **14** *consort* concert   **19** *sweet-tongued Greek* Greek orator Demosthenes, who overcame a speech defect
25 *obnoxious* vulnerable   **32** *those nine* the muses

A Letter to her Husband
Simon Bradstreet was a member of the General Court at Boston
4 *Ipswich* forty miles north of Boston   **12** *Capricorn* the sun is in Capricorn in mid-winter   **21** *Cancer* Cancer is the first sign of summer

Another Song
8 *Ver* spring   **60** conjectured: the last line is missing

An excuse for so much writ upon my Verses
1 *coil* fuss

Natures Cook
11 *pox* small-pox might leave the skin minced-looking, but French suggests syphilis   **13** *calentures* delirious fevers   **20** *megrims* migraines

A Dissert
4 *marchpane* marzipan   **9** *green-sickness* adolescent anaemia

Of the Animal Spirits
These were subtle, refined substances, believed to permeate and animate the body and blood.

The Fort or Castle of Hope
9 *pia-mater* membrane enclosing the brain

Friendship's Mystery, to my dearest Lucasia
The dedicatee was Anne Lewis, later Owen, named for a character in William Cartwright's play *The Lady Errant* (1636)

Epitaph on her Son H.P.
He died in 1655.   **16** *Hermes' seal* Hermetic seal, named for
Hermes Trismegistus, derived from the Egyptian god associated
with alchemy

Lucasia, Rosania and Orinda parting at a Fountain, July 1663
Possibly mis-dated or fictitious. 'Rosania', a childhood friend,
Mary Aubrey, became 'apostate' by marrying in 1652; 'Lucasia'
married, and moved to Ireland in 1662

The Disappointment
122 *the Delphic god* Apollo, god of poetry   **129** *her love was slain*
Adonis, killed by a boar

To Alexis in Answer to his Poem against Fruition
The title refers to the preceding poem in the collection *Lycidus*.
5 *beboches* trivial vanities?

To the fair Clarinda
23 the union of Hermes and Aphrodite (here three syllables)
produced the hermaphrodite

To a Proud Beauty
20 *nice* foolishly affected; *kind* unsophisticated

In the Person of a Lady
37 *and then* text reads 'than'

On a picture Painted by her self
1 *Diana* goddess of chastity and hunting

Upon the saying that my verses were made by another
12 *holocaust* burnt offering   **24** *empale* surround   **35** *Aesop's
painted jay* in one of Aesop's fables, a jay dresses in peacock's
feathers, and is mobbed by other birds   **47** *Orinda* Katherine
Philips   **63** *Cassandra* cursed by Apollo, so that her prophecies
would not be believed

The Introduction
25 *glad day* the Israelites' celebration of the bringing of the Ark of the Covenant into Jerusalem   **35** *bright chorus* the Israelite women greeted the victorious David with songs   **45** *a woman here* the judge Deborah led the Israelites to victory, and then composed a triumph song

The Spleen
2 *Proteus* the shape-changing sea-god

The Unequal Fetters
18 *Hymen* the god of marriage

A Nocturnal Reverie
19 *Salisbury* Anne Tufton, Countess of Salisbury

The Female Advocate
1 *How canst thou think* referring to Robert Gould, in *Love Giv'n O're* (1682)

The Liberty
8 *round circle* necromancer's chalk circle, drawn to confine spirits
34 *closet* small study   **36** old romance, *The Seven Champions of Christendom*   **42** *Probatum est* note of efficacy of medicine

The Emulation
12 *Pentateuch* the first five books of the Old Testament   **36** *ten celestial females* presumably the nine muses and their mother, Mnemosyne   **37** *two gods* Apollo and Dionysus

To one that persuades me to leave the Muses
4 *Hundred's* parish rate or tax   **41** *Japan* Japan-work, painting or enamelling   **42** *glass* hand-painted mirrors

A Paraphrase on the Canticles: II
31 *Pindarics* the irregular odes of Pindar

Six Town Eclogues
19 *the Ring* in Hyde Park, used for social parade   **21** *Lilly,*

Motteux shopkeepers   **34** *overseen the card* underwritten her next bet   **66** *pomatums* ointments   **75** *Galen* named for the famous classical physician   **77***Machaon* named for the doctor-hero of Garth's poem *The Dispensary* (1699)

The Lover
2 *Molly* her friend May Skerrett, Sir Robert Walpole's mistress

'Between your sheets'
10 *Lindamira* Francesco Algarotti

The Womans Labour
1 *Immortal Bard!* Stephen Duck, to whose *The Thresher's Labour* this is a response   **2** *Caroline* Queen Caroline, who gave him a pension   **34** *Alcides' labours* labours of Hercules   **234** *wort* liquid for brewing

Fair and Softly goes far
34 *Eringo roots* sea-holly root, believed to be an aphrodisiac
56 *cunctando* delaying   **76** Richard Blackmore, poet and physician, and Sir Hans Soane, physician   **93** *Grotius* seventeenth-century scholar   **111** *Warwick-lane* centre of the medical profession

The Sacrifice
16 *Parnassian deities* Mount Parnassus was sacred to the nine Muses

Mira's Will
27 *virtuoso* the learned, especially in the arts

An Epistle to Lady Bowyer
16 *rappee* a coarse kind of snuff   **26** *Cornus* Pope's name for a cuckold   **44** *Maid of Honour* the Honourable Miss Lovelace (Mary Jones's note)

Washing-Day
2 *the buskined step* the tragic mode   **38** *Erebus* the classical underworld   **82** the Montgolfier brothers invented the balloon; first flight in 1783

The Rights of Woman
Mary Wollstonecraft's *Vindication of the Rights of Women* was
published in 1792

Verses Inviting Mrs C— to Tea
34 'See the Dying Indian in Dodsley's poems: "The dart of Isdabel
prevails! 'twas dipt / In double poison".' (Scott's note)   **40** *bitter
tea* the Boston 'Tea-Party', 1773   **41** *Ate* spirit of malevolence
or vengeance   **52** 'Alluding to Captain Donellan's murder of
Sir Theodosius Boughton by laurel-water' (Scott's note)

Colebrook Dale
6 *them* Naiads, water-nymphs   **10** *Sabrina* spirit of the River
Severn   **12** *Cyclops* Vulcan's malformed foundry-man
50 *ponderous metal* iron ore

Invocation, to the Genius of Slumber
8 Honora Sneyd, her adopted sister, d.1781   **54** drawing a
silhouette

The Bas Bleu
22 *orgeat* cooling drink of almonds and orange-flower water

The Riot
76 *mittimus* a prison warrant

Thirty-eight
44 *myrtle* sacred to Venus   **46** *amaranth* legendary unfading
flower   **47** *Minerva* goddess of wisdom

Recreation
47 the Duke of Brunswick died fighting Napoleon at Quatre Bras,
1815

Sonnets from the Portuguese: V
2 see Sophocles' *Electra*; a guilty memory of her brother Edward,
drowned in 1840   **12** *Beloved* the poet Robert Browning

To George Sand
The pseudonym of Amandine Dupin, Baronne Dudevant
(1804-76), French writer and feminist

Casa Guidi Windows
Casa Guidi was the Brownings' home in Florence, whence she
watched the uprising against the Duke, 1849

Stanzas
This poem is sometimes attributed to Charlotte Brontë

High Tide on the Coast of Lincolnshire
28 *melic* a pasture grass

In an Artist's Studio
The artist is Dante Gabriel Rossetti, the model is Elizabeth Siddal

Among His Books
34 *Elzevir* family of Dutch printers, issued beautiful editions of
the classics 1592-1681   **35** *Aldine* from the Venetian printer
Aldus Manutius, who specialized in the Greek and Roman
classics in the late fifteenth-early sixteenth centuries

Index of First Lines

Deep, and silent, and wide 237
Did I boast of liberty 50
Did I intend my lines for public view 99
Does the road wind up-hill all the way 230
Down a broad river of the western wilds 195
Dream that stole o'er us in the time 208

Fair lovely maid, or if that title be 85
False hope, which feeds but to destroy, and spill 48
Farewell (sweet Cookeham) where I first obtained 39
Forbear, bold youth, all Heaven's here 73
Forgo the Muses! No, in spite 116
Friendship, as some sage poet sings 175

Great Nature she doth clothe the soul within 64
Green is the plane-tree in the square 250
Grey the sky, and growing dimmer 235

Here, here are our enjoyments done 75
Her even lines her steady temper show 156
High waving heather 'neath stormy blasts bending 211
How far are they deceived, that hope in vain 93
How like her! But 'tis she herself 251
How long, great God, a wretched captive here 115
How much of paper's spoiled! what floods of ink 151

I ask not wit, nor beauty do I crave 137
I can't, Celinda, say, I love 114
I did not live until this time 72
I grieve and dare not show my discontent 21
I heard last night a little child go singing 199
I lift my heavy heart up solemnly 197
I must not think of thee; and, tired yet strong 240
I once was happy, when while yet a child 175
I sat before my glass one day 252
I think I see my father's sister stand 200
I think of thee! – my thoughts do twine and bud 198